UNDERSTANDING
MICHAEL S. HARPER

UNDERSTANDING CONTEMPORARY AMERICAN LITERATURE
Matthew J. Bruccoli, Founding Editor
Linda Wagner-Martin, Series Editor

Also of Interest

Understanding Adrienne Rich, Jeannette E. Riley
Understanding Alice Walker, Thadious M. Davis
Understanding August Wilson, Mary L. Bogumil
Understanding Colson Whitehead, Derek C. Maus
Understanding Edward P. Jones, James W. Coleman
Understanding Etheridge P. Knight, Michael S. Collins
Understanding James Baldwin, Marc Dudley
Understanding John Edgar Wideman, D. Quentin Miller
Understanding Randall Kenan, Andy Crank
Understanding Sharon Olds, Russell Brickey

UNDERSTANDING

MICHAEL S. HARPER

Michael Antonucci

THE UNIVERSITY OF
SOUTH CAROLINA PRESS

© 2023 University of South Carolina

Published by the University of South Carolina Press
Columbia, South Carolina 29208

www.uscpress.com

Manufactured in the United States of America

32 31 30 29 28 27 26 25 24 23
10 9 8 7 6 5 4 3 2 1

Library of Congress Cataloging-in-Publication Data
can be found at http://catalog.loc.gov/.

ISBN: 978-1-64336-399-8 (hardcover)
ISBN: 978-1-64336-400-1 (paperback)
ISBN: 978-1-64336-401-8 (ebook)

CONTENTS

SERIES EDITOR'S PREFACE

The Understanding Contemporary American Literature series was founded by the estimable Matthew J. Bruccoli (1931–2008), who envisioned these volumes as guides or companions for students as well as good nonacademic readers, a legacy that will continue as new volumes are developed to fill in gaps among the nearly one hundred series volumes published to date and to embrace a host of new writers only now making their marks on our literature.

As Professor Bruccoli explained in his preface to the volumes he edited, because much influential contemporary literature makes special demands, "the word *understanding* in the titles was chosen deliberately. Many willing readers lack an adequate understanding of how contemporary literature works; that is, of what the author is attempting to express and the means by which it is conveyed." Aimed at fostering this understanding of good literature and good writers, the criticism and analysis in the series provide instruction in how to read certain contemporary writers—explicating their material, language, structures, themes, and perspectives—and facilitate a more profitable experience of the works under discussion.

In the twenty-first century Professor Bruccoli's prescience gives us an avenue to publish expert critiques of significant contemporary American writing. The series continues to map the literary landscape and to provide both instruction and enjoyment. Future volumes will seek to introduce new voices alongside canonized favorites, to chronicle the changing literature of our times, and to remain, as Professor Bruccoli conceived, contemporary in the best sense of the word.

Linda Wagner-Martin, Series Editor

ACKNOWLEDGMENTS

Completing a project such as this requires attention, support, and time. These resources have arrived in various ways, and I am grateful for them all. Acknowledgments and appreciations are due to Aurora Bell and the University of South Carolina Press, Professor Thadious Davis, as well as the Harper family. Thank you for your patience.

Thanks also go to Elizabeth Alexander, Jeffery Renard Allen, Herman Beavers, Kimberly W. Benston, Jonathan Blunk, Garin Cycholl, Elizabeth Dodd, Sara Ellis, Elizabeth Muther, Xavier Nicholas, Robert B. Stepto, Ron Sharpe, Ed Pavlic, Heather Treseler, Judith Vollmer, Lucia Vilankulu, Anthony Walton, John Wright, and John Zheng for their assistance and council.

The project is indebted to long-standing commitments made by Dwight A. Andrews, Mark A. Sanders, and the late Rudolph P. Byrd.

This manuscript would not have been possible without the guidance of Afaa M. Weaver, Duriel E. Harris, Frances Smith Foster, and Sterling D. Plumpp.

Finally, these words and pages were produced with concerted energies generously given by my family, Ernesto Victor Antonucci and Madeline Fan: "A LOVE SUPREME."

CHAPTER 1

Understanding Michael S. Harper

Michael S. Harper delivers a set of detailed poetic commentaries on Black experience in the United States through the course of his eleven volumes of published verse. Bringing attention to questions concerning history, kinship, and geography, Harper's literary project recognizes Black people and Black culture as simultaneously informing, challenging, and expanding conceptions of American identity. In a body of work produced over five decades, Harper's poetry explores Black expressive tradition, treating music, literature, and the visual arts as an archive of Black life, Black thought, and Black culture. Entering these conversations, examining questions of memory and belonging, Harper's verse assembles a distinct set of perspectives on Black America and the American experience writ large.

Throughout his body of work, Harper traces movements and patterns he observes at, along, and across the American color line. Mapping the contours of this boundary, his poetry recognizes Blackness and people of African descent as significant contributors to the development of American culture. Embracing complication and attending to disparities emerging from the contested space that his work explores, the poet effectively pursues a literary discussion of American complexity. His poetry records images and presents impressions of Black life in the African diaspora. As such, Harper's verse presents a counternarrative to white supremacist mythologies about the composition and origins of the United States, reshaping prevailing discourse about race, nation, and identity.

To undertake this project, Harper's poetry employs a fluid, inclusive ("both/and") approach to the subject matter it treats. Assuming this position, the poet's body of work resists, even defies, simple classification. With these "both/and" engagements informing the structure and content of Harper's verse, the poet delivers a set of varied, conjoined, multivocal presentations and representations of *both* Black experience *and* American culture. As these impulses coalesce and inform his project, the poet demonstrates a sustained commitment to resisting reductive binaries. Harper's body of work thereby restructures common assumptions and established understandings about "American" subjects. For some readers, revising and revisiting "ordinary" components of American life—raising questions about citizenship, geography, home and work spaces, arts and entertainment as it does—the poet's verse creates "confusion" and/or becomes "difficult" to process. Anthony Walton addresses these possibilities in "The Hardheaded Romantic," his reading of Harper's late-career praise poem "Ghost of Soul Making."

Dedicated to Krystallnacht survivor Ruth Oppenheim, a long-time Brown University English Department administrator and valued colleague of Harper's, "Ghost of Soul Making" explores the "both/and" ambiguities that inform the poet's project. In his discussion of the work, Walton suggests that "Harper's poems have grown ever more complex and inclusive" ("The Hardheaded Romantic," 49). Incorporating open-ended, double-edged lines and phrases such as "At birth, and before" and "where answers do not answer" into "Ghost of Soul Making," the poet supports this reading. According to critic George Steiner, oblique, equivocal poetic gestures, such as these, "confound" readers by generating "difficulty."

Examining this dynamic in his essay "On Difficulty," Steiner brings perspective to the "both/and" approach Harper employs throughout his verse. The critic argues that whether readers are attempting to understand an individual poem or a poet's entire project, they attempt to form specific connections with the work. Suggesting that this process unfolds by "virtue of knowledge and archeology of feeling," he claims that audiences develop connections with a poem through "reconstructive acquaintance" (269). Conversely, Steiner also makes the case that when readers are unable to familiarize themselves with a poem or body of poetic work, they experience what he calls "authentic apprehension" (269). In this way, a reader's ability to "grasp" a poem determines whether it is "difficult" to process.

"On Difficulty" opens with Steiner posing a deceptively simple question: "What do we mean when we say: This poem or this passage in this poem is *difficult*?" The critic suggests that there is a difference between the difficulties involved in interpreting a poetic passage and those invested in "an argument in Immanuel Kant or [a] theorem in Algebra" (263). Qualifying his claim, Steiner identifies four distinct types of poetic difficulty: "*contingent* difficulty," "*modal* difficulty," "*tactical* difficulty," and "*ontological* difficulty." "Contingent difficulty" is the by-product of verse that requires readers to "do their homework" and/or "look it up" (267); "modal difficulty" emanates from a poem's use of referents and foundational structures; "tactical difficulties" is more "intentional," manifest by or through "the writer's will" (270). "Ontological difficulty" emerges from questions of "meaning" that lead audiences to inquire "for whom the poet . . . is writing, [or] publishing?" (275).

If Steiner's "On Difficulty" is used as a framework for examining Harper's poetry, the poet's body of work exhibits "modal difficulties" that, according to the critic, "lie with the beholder" (270). Considered from this perspective, the difficult aspects of Harper's poetry do not emerge from *what it is* as much as *what it isn't*. Put another way, the poet's verse "confuses" some readers because of what it doesn't do, rather than what it actually does. According to Steiner, readers come to understand difficult poetry, such as Harper's, by exploring the "modal" limits of the poetry and adjusting their own "penetrative inscape" (269). The critic suggests that, in order to gain a better sense of difficult verse, readers allow themselves to "understand at the cerebral level, the dynamics of judgment" and recognize "that [they] cannot coerce [their] own sensibility into the relevant frame of perception" (269).

Steiner's essay offers a way to initiate productive readings of poetic projects such as Harper's. The critic's extended discussion of "difficult poetry" effectively presents "modal difficulty" as a means of reconciling the confusion and contradictions some readers experience when they encounter the "both/and" impulses found in Harper's body of work. Inviting readers to reduce their "distance" from the poet's verse, Steiner constructs an almost paradoxical mechanism for comprehending "difficult poetry," recognizing the work's "difference" as informing its "difficulty." Applying terms and interpretive approaches from Steiner's essay to Harper's verse in this way ultimately creates a method for understanding difficulty and difference in the poet's work, situating it within conversations concerned with both Black letters and American letters writ large.

Published in 1978, "On Difficulty" provides a snapshot of a critical literary discussion taking place as Harper reached one of many milestones during his lengthy career. Steiner's work appeared as *Images of Kin,* Harper's first volume of new and collected poems, was receiving high praise, having been named as a finalist for that year's National Book Award in poetry as well as receiving the Melville Cane Award. "On Difficulty" presents a critical approach to Harper's reputation for producing "difficult poetry" grounded in the moment. Providing insight into the poet's work and its relationship with this label, Steiner speaks to Harper's profile as a "well-known" and "well-respected" poet whose verse is, ultimately, not well-understood. "On Difficulty" effectively facilitates discussion of the poet's work in terms of its contradictory status as being

"under-examined" despite having received acclaim across many literary categories, including Black letters, American poetry, and international poetics.

By examining Harper's body of work in these terms, the poet's project
appears to be the recipient of more celebration than substantive critical discussion. This observation gains credence by bringing consideration to the attention it's garnered through engaging with Black expressive tradition, especially
Black music. For example, while Harper's poetic portraits of Black artists and
their work are widely hailed, his poetry's connections to the lore and lived experience informing Black expression—particularly jazz and blues—is seldom
discussed. Similarly, Harper's demonstrated commitment to examining questions of history in his verse has brought generous praise to his work throughout his career. Yet his active use of individualized and family-based accounts
of Black experience in his literary explorations of historical subjects remains
largely unrecognized. The subdued response given to this aspect of his verse
resembles the critical discussion that has greeted Harper's effort to integrate
traditional Black knowledge into his poetic project.

By exploring overlooked and under-examined areas of Harper's verse,
this study seeks to clarify and develop a more complete understanding of the
poet and his body of work. This study looks to process the "modal difficulty"
Harper's poetry generates, while reducing the "contingent difficulty" that some
readers experience through their engagements with his work. To do so, I introduce the terms "generative kinship" and "convergent history" into this discussion of Harper's poetry, building on criticism by Robert Stepto, John Callahan,
and others and using these terms to speak to the "difficulty" of the poet's verse
and its capacity to "confound" (Steiner's word) some audiences.

Generative kinship and convergent history serve as critical frameworks for
my engagement with Harper's body of work. These terms contextualize the
lives and experiences of family members and other notable figures that the
poet considers through his literary survey of Black America and the American
experience. In this way, kinship and history act as signposts within the study,
addressing various types of "difficulty" that emerge from the allusions and imagery in Harper's poetry. Extending the scope of critical discussions concerned
with Harper's verse, the project seeks to expand the poet's circle of readers,
promote a broader understanding of his body of work, and establish its place
within both Black letters and American poetry.

These objectives are premised on the belief that convergent history and
generative kinship are connective threads that the poet invests throughout his
poetic project. Understood as common points of engagement, these categories enhance continuities between Harper's earlier poems and verse published
during the later phases of his career. The concepts "convergent history" and

"generative kinship" strengthen the connections and thus promote discussion of verse written and published by the poet after 1978. Treating work from the middle and later stages of Harper's career in this way, I aim to effectively establish a dialogue between the poet's earlier, more familiar poems and his lesser known, "difficult" later works.

The First Six

Recognizing that much of what has been said and written about Harper's poetic project is rooted—almost exclusively—in discussions of verse from his first six volumes, I offer an alternative approach to considering his body of work. In this study, I effectively reframe prevailing critical conversations, presenting poems from "the first six" as a chronicle of Harper's experiences between 1970 and 1977, in which a little-known Black poet from the West Coast established his voice within American letters. The study thus regards the work he published during this prolific seven-year period—*Dear John, Dear Coltrane* (1970), *History Is Your Own Heartbeat* (1971), *Song: I Want a Witness* (1972), *Debridement* (1973), *Nightmare Begins Responsibility* (1975), and *Images of Kin* (1977)—as establishing the foundation of Harper's literary profile. Poems from these volumes earned the poet a list of awards and accolades, including National Book Award nominations in 1970 and 1977 along with the 1972 Black Academy of Arts and Letters Award for poetry, a Guggenheim Fellowship in 1976, and fellowships from the National Endowment for the Arts, along with the Poetry Society of America's 1978 Melville Cane Award.

The influence of Harper's first six volumes on discussions of the poet and his body of work cannot be underestimated. As such, this study brings poems from those volumes into conversation with the entirety of his project as it refines and revises understandings of his verse and its place within both Black letters and American poetry. Working toward these ends, my discussion recognizes that poems Harper published between 1970 and 1977 have sustained the interest of literary critics across multiple generations. For example, in his groundbreaking 1973 study *Understanding the New Black Poetry*, Stephen E. Henderson discusses the title poem from Harper's first collection of published verse, "Dear John, Dear Coltrane." Identifying the correspondence between Harper's poem and "the companion poem that Coltrane wrote for the [*A Love Supreme*] album," Henderson understands the poet's work as conjuring the saxophonist's project by "building upon the phrase 'a love supreme'" and "suggesting a musician improvising" (49).

Writing some thirty years later, Elizabeth Alexander also explores Harper's "Dear John, Dear Coltrane" in her essay "I Am a Black Man: Michael Harper's Black Aesthetic." Like Henderson, Alexander acknowledges Harper's poem as being infused by Coltrane's voice and a jazz sensibility. She notes that the poet effectively becomes Coltrane as he "sings the essential refrain 'a love supreme' when the poem is performed" (73). Alexander discusses the poem in terms of its double-inflected twoness: "Harper is Coltrane with history, politics, and anger; where Coltrane mourns, Harper rages" (73). Comparing Henderson and Alexander's readings of "Dear John, Dear Coltrane," it becomes evident that despite the notoriety and distinction that Harper's poetry gained between 1973 and 2004, critical discussions about his work, in many ways, remained bound to poems from his first six volumes and a string of associations focusing on these works' engagements with jazz, history, and poetic portraiture.

The persistent, sustained interest in Harper's earlier work ultimately creates a dynamic that has, in some ways, impeded fresh readings and fuller understandings of his verse. As such, the poet and his project have been oddly consumed, at least in part, by their own success. In an effort to break this cycle, I draw upon the numerous literary interviews that Harper granted over the course of his career. By doing so, the poet is allowed to "speak for himself" and reframe a portion of the critical conversation about his work while addressing some of the difficulty associated with his body of work. For instance, in his 1987 interview with James R. Keegan, Harper speaks to his poetry's engagement with Black experience in the United States: "For me the story of black [sic] people in this country is the essential story . . . I think the special calling of black [sic] writers is to demonstrate the complexity of black [sic] characterization. . . . as a trustee of the American idiom, I feel an obligation to my own sense of style, poignance, and compassion." ("History, Heartbeat, and Jazz"). This study devotes attention to the poet's efforts to reframe prevailing notions about Black life and American culture in order to make his project more accessible to his readers.

Connecting verse from Harper's earlier poems to work found in his later collections, this study follows critical pathways that Judith Vollmer blazed in a talk she delivered during the 2013 Michael S. Harper festival, held at the University of Missouri. Vollmer frames her discussion of Harper's poetry, which she describes as including "interior backlit spaces" and "geometric natural landscapes," as providing audiences with "a visual field-stage and historical narrative" ("Weather, Sundials, and Other Time Machines," 3). Vollmer traces the features and contours that she locates upon this poetic terrain, identifying a complex set of literary undertakings that Harper's project pursues. She understands his verse as surveying areas of American experience that would otherwise remain "under examined" or "overlooked." She identifies the receptivity of Harper's "swiftly absorbing 'open' composition," as his literary project's prevailing quality (3).

Vollmer sees the poet and his verse as sketching a broader, more inclusive American cultural landscape. She compares Harper's verse to works by Black Mountain poets that she also regards as "demonstrat[ing] a consistent commitment [to] 'practitioners of open field' strategies." Vollmer notes, however, that Harper's poems "construct intimate spaces in his verse . . . on a more human scale," identifying their capacity for "creating a sensation that . . . resonate[s] in the way [a] singer, storyteller, whisperer, or secret messenger might utter the historical record, piece by piece" (3). As such, Harper's poems feel "warmer" and "closer" than those of Black Mountain school poets; she locates the deeply felt, personal experiences which inform Harper's verse as it charts both individualized and collective movements along an axis of co-constructive engagement.

The Poet, His Poems, and Kin

Michael Steven Harper, first child born to Walter Warren Harper, a United States Postal Service worker, and Katherine Louise Johnson, a medical stenographer, was born on March 18, 1938, delivered by the hands of his maternal grandfather, Canadian-born physician Dr. Rolland Johnson, in the Bedford-Stuyvesant neighborhood of Brooklyn, New York. The circumstances of his arrival—a home birth in the multistory residential building located at 908 Lafayette Avenue, owned by Dr. Johnson—underscores the exceptional position Harper's family occupied within Black America as it was constituted prior to World War II.[1] Writing in "My Poetic Technique and the Humanization of the American Audience," Harper explains: "there was much lore attached to my birth, much signifying" (27). Throughout this mid-career autobiographical reflection and poetic manifesto, Harper delivers an account of his upbringing, explaining that his "poetic technique" was shaped by the combination of persistent good fortune and sustained familial support that defined his early years.

At the outset of the essay, Harper writes: "My parents weren't rich, but they had a good record collection, and they prohibited me from playing any of their 78's, which was a guarantee that I'd investigate in my own time, always when they were out of the house" (28). Assembling images and collecting insights drawn from his early years, "My Poetic Technique" constructs a vivid collage of material drawn from a range of subjects that includes ancestry, lineage, and belonging. Examining events from Harper's Brooklyn childhood, "My Poetic Technique" delivers an impressionistic account of the poet's development as an artist, focusing on family and connections, punctuated by "music and trains."

Read as a guided tour of Harper's verse, the essay ultimately provides insight into the poet's distinct understanding of kinship and historical connections. Speaking to the relationships that he maintains with figures who populate his poetic project, "My Poetic Technique" situates Harper's body of work within an expansive discussion of personal experiences and their defining contexts, offering a detailed account of the poet's engagement with historical, musical, and folkloric subjects. At the same time, this brief, impressionistic, autobiographical essay also becomes a site where Harper sifts through the fallout of his family's decision to leave Brooklyn and relocate to Los Angeles during the summer of 1951.

At its basic level, "My Poetic Technique" recognizes that, when the poet's father accepted a transfer to the United States Postal Service's Terminal Annex in Los Angeles, the cross-country move disrupted the foundations of what Harper regarded as his world. While the relocation obviously impacted the poet's relationships to members of his close-knit extended family on Lafayette Avenue, the move to California ultimately recast Harper's ambitions to attend Stuyvesant High School—the prestigious New York City public high school, where he'd gained admission—and to pursue a career in medicine. These academic and professional goals were gradually eclipsed as soon as the poet entered the Los Angeles public school system, where he was greeted by a particularly dogged brand of institutional racism.

Despite his record of high academic achievement in the New York Public Schools, when Harper enrolled at Dorsey High School in Los Angeles he was placed in the school's industrial arts track. In "My Poetic Technique," the poet recalls a similar mid-twentieth-century Los Angeles educational experience: "I learned a little terminology from a zoology teacher in Los Angeles who had us count somites in his worms. He told me I shouldn't study because I would never get into medical school; I should pick up a broom and forget the microscope" (30). This racist piece of career advice was given to the poet at Los Angeles City College. Ultimately, the zoology teacher's comments pushed Harper out of the biology lab and into City College's English Department.

After completing an Associate of Arts degree in English, Harper transferred to Los Angeles State College in 1959, committing himself to literary studies. In "My Poetic Technique," Harper explains that while attending classes at Los Angeles State, he worked at the Post Office and enjoyed the time he spent with his Black co-workers. Fondly recalling the deep, intercultural literacy of his Post Office cohort, Harper refers to the postal facing table—his USPS workstation—as "the [Black] middle-class equivalent to the pool hall": "almost everyone in sight had advanced degrees . . . it was there that I learned about Tolsoi [sic] and So What Dostoevsky, as one of my partners used to call the Russian underground man" (28).

Taking these workplace conversations to heart, Harper incorporated them into his studies at Los Angeles State. Reading voraciously and writing both poetry and fiction, he worked closely with the English Department's writing faculty, which included poet Henri Coulette, novelist Wirt Williams, and fiction writer Christopher Isherwood. After graduating from Los Angeles State College with a Bachelor of Arts degree in 1961, Harper applied to the graduate program at the University of Iowa. Receiving support and encouragement from his faculty mentors in the English Department, Harper was admitted to the prestigious Iowa Writers' Workshop at mid-year, traveling to Iowa City to begin his coursework in January 1962. Harper's transition from Los Angeles to snowy Iowa City was a memorably unpleasant experience. In addition to his dislike for the cold, midwestern winter weather, the poet found the near complete absence of Black people and Black culture to be especially challenging.

Harper became increasingly alienated by the racial dynamics he experienced both within the workshop and away from campus: "I was the only [Black student] in either fiction or poetry and I was enrolled in both. Several teachers asked me was I going to be another James Baldwin—one of our faculty members was so obsessed with Baldwin he knew I'd known Mr. Baldwin" ("My Poetic Technique," 29). Describing his attempt to clarify his relationship with Baldwin to his professor, Harper writes that he tried to let him know that "I had read Baldwin's novels and essays, but hadn't met him personally." However, the poet's appeal to reason was pushed aside by the persistent capacity of white supremacy to simplify, distort, and misunderstand. Ultimately, feeling compelled to fight fire with fire, he "began to specialize in retorts to affronts. You met Isaac Singer? You been hunting with Hemingway? But this kind of humor didn't go over very well" (29).

Confronting the sense of alienation that he experienced while among the white professors and the majority of students in his Workshop courses, Harper recalls the relief he found when he "hung out with the [Black] football players during the era of Iowa's great dynasty" (29). By "dancing to 'Gypsy Woman' and playing tonk in the Black athletes' housing" (29), Harper voluntarily removed himself from the scramble to establish his place within the Workshop's pecking order. In this way, the poet developed a strategy for self-preservation in Iowa City that he would use throughout his professional career.

Despite the deep ambivalence that Harper expresses about his Workshop experiences in "My Poetic Technique," his time in Iowa City undoubtedly provided an opportunity to develop and refine his poetic voice. In his detailed biographical discussion of Harper and his career, "The Hardheaded Romantic," Anthony Walton explains: "it was at Iowa that Harper began to write the poems which would constitute his celebrated first volume, *Dear John, Dear Coltrane*" (46). Walton cites a passage from "Brother John"—the first poem found in the volume that launched Harper's career:

> *I'm black; I am—*
> *A black man; black—*
> *I'm a black man;*
> *I'm a black man;*
> *I'm a man; black—*
> *I am* (46)

Praising the passage and its "compelling rhythms," Walton identifies "the I of the poet," embarking on "a journey" that "comes to celebrate the self" (46). He goes on to explain that the poem becomes "all the more remarkable," recognizing that these lines were composed by "a young man sitting through the wind, snow and ice of a bleak Iowa winter and by force of imagination working toward this new transcendence" (46).

Harper would ultimately complete his graduate work at the University of Iowa in 1964. After submitting his master's thesis, "Blues and Laughter," to his advisor Donald Justice, the poet returned to Los Angeles where he taught English at Pasadena College while living at his parents' home. Eventually, Harper made his way to San Francisco, having secured a teaching position at Contra Costa College. While writing, teaching, and digging a mid-'60s Bay Area music scene dedicated to improvisation and the principles of "free expression," Harper became acquainted with Shirley Buffington, a white woman from Minnesota who had recently relocated to California and was staying with relatives in the East Bay. Harper and Buffington's relationship continued to grow and in December 1965, they married. In 1966 Shirley gave birth to the couple's first son, Rolland Warren Harper, in San Francisco. Rolland's arrival established a foundational component of the "well-knit family" Harper writes about in his 1971 poem, "Here Where Coltrane Is." The couple would go on to have four other children—Ruben Maasai and Michael Steven, who died shortly after their birth, as well as Patrice Cuchulain and Rachel Maria, who survived—before their marriage ended in divorce in 1998.

A Love Supreme

Throughout Harper's body of work, in poems like "Here Where Coltrane Is," the music and persona of John Coltrane repeatedly emerges as a means by which the poet accesses and examines both generative kinship and convergent history within his poetic project. Coltrane serves as both a source of inspiration for the poet and a mode by which he explores territories where identity, space, and experience intersect. Kimberly W. Benston's essay "Harper and Trane: Modal Enactments of 'A Love Supreme'" considers connections linking the poet to the musician and the relationship that Harper cultivates with

Coltrane's artistic legacies. It presents the musician as an aesthetic trailblazer and spiritual guide for Black artists, acknowledging the exonerated place that Trane holds among Black cultural practitioners.

Benston suggests that the title poem to Harper's first volume of verse, "Dear John, Dear Coltrane," offers the "most striking instance of [Harper's] engagement with music and Trane" (41). Understanding the poem as an example of the "complex struggle of black [sic] expressive modernism" that Harper engages throughout his verse, he suggests that it underscores the poet's "commitment to an interchange of multiple voices within a contradictory landscape of death and renewal" (41). As such, Benston's essay effectively identifies where Coltrane's status as a Black artist intersects with the essential concerns of Harper's poetic project; the poem's "remarkable elegy's dialectic of change and affirmation, bereavement and love" renders a "particular and complex set of connections" (41).

Making this claim, Benston effectively identifies the call/response ethos that he sees informing Harper's poetic project. His essay draws on a quote from the writer's statement that Harper prepared for Tom Weatherly and Tim Wilenz's *Natural Process: An Anthology of New Black Poetry*. Asserting that "my poems are modal," Harper writes that his work seeks "to revivify and regenerate, spiritually, man [sic] and community" (43). Amplifying on these sentiments, Benston writes that within the poet's verse, "'Coltrane,' therefore, will stand as the name of this crossing of autonomous and collective experience" (44). The critic thus affirms Harper's contention that "the blues singer says 'I' but the audience assumes 'We'; out of such energy comes community and freedom" (Weatherly and Wilenz, 43).

Benston suggests that in the course of "Dear John, Dear Coltrane," readers see the poet invest its "titular hero [with] the *respon*sibility of locating the modal link between the individual artist's tragic isolation and the community's 'regenerative' perception" (44, emphasis in original). In "Harper and Trane," the poet uses the chant "A Love Supreme" as a means of affirming what the critic calls the "'testament' imperative of Coltrane's art" (45). According to Benston, when Harper deploys the chant in "Dear John, Dear Coltrane," he becomes connected to the "touchstone of spiritual commitment through which [Coltrane] declared publicly the sacramental quest to which his art was thereafter openly dedicated" (45).

Benston suggests that the call/response pattern found in "Dear John, Dear Coltrane" is one that the poet engages throughout his body of work. Harper's verse contacts "the interior dynamic of search and renovation with which Coltrane's work had always been concerned. . . ." (45). Regarding the poet's literary explorations of the Coltrane legacy and articulation of "a love supreme" in this way, Benston depicts the poet delivering an amplified imprint of the musician's aesthetic project. Harper's verse conducts a series of poetic memory acts and performance rituals. Through these invocations of Coltrane and his music, the poet works to renew and reframe dialogues concerned with Black experience and Black expression both in the United States and across the African diaspora.

According to Benston, this sense of consolidation and exchange within Coltrane's *oeuvre* becomes fully evident in the collection of musical recordings that has come to us as the album entitled *A Love Supreme*. In "Harper and Trane," the critic describes *A Love Supreme*—from its cover design to its musical execution and recording production—as "the most tightly integrated conceptions among all of Coltrane's late compositions" (45). Connecting the structure of the four-part suite to the lengthy "annunciation poem" that the musician wrote and included as the album's liner notes, Benston praises the "modal interdisciplinarity" of Coltrane's project. He continues by writing that "*A Love Supreme* insinuates call-and-response as a thematic and structural principle, fashioning a plethora of conversations between vertical and harmonic patterns, while connecting the segments across their disparate coloristic values through many echoes of pitch and statement" (46). Considering Harper's sustained pursuit of aesthetic resonance with Coltrane and his quartet in this way, Benston's study offers reflections on these foundational exchanges between poet and musician.

For Coltrane and the members of his "classic quartet," *A Love Supreme* stands as a musical statement on spirituality, creative process, renewal, and an affirmation of transcendent possibilities. As a suite written in four parts ("Acknowledgment," "Resolution," "Pursuance," and "Psalm"), the composition moves into the distinct spaces that the musicians create. Benston writes that the texture of *A Love Supreme* is shaped by "musical and verbal improvisations," thereby providing audiences and artists with an opportunity to "rethink the tragic contingencies of lived reality by displacing homogenous, punctiform duration with a felt sense of time as multidirectional *passage*" (48, emphasis in original). The imprint of Coltrane, his music, and the aesthetic directions that he and his collaborators articulate as "a love supreme" is evident throughout Harper's poetic project. Recognizing that the musician and his work form a sustained presence for the poet and his verse, this study is organized as a reflection of the four movements that comprise Coltrane's *A Love Supreme*.

The study begins with "Acknowledgment (Kinship)" (chapter 2), which examines Harper's poetic engagements with kin and kinship as thematic concepts. Building on a foundation of critical and scholarly works by Robert B. Stepto, John F. Callahan, and Michael Cooke, the chapter brings consideration to the way aesthetic bonds and ethical alignments construct "family" throughout the poet's body of work. "Acknowledgment" understands Harper's use of "generative kinship" as a primary conduit connecting the poet to his subject matter. Family, kinship, and ancestry are acknowledged as lenses for discussing four poems from the poet's "first six" volumes—"Grandfather, "Here Where Coltrane Is," "Last Affair," and "Alice"—along with one lesser known poem, "Goin' to the Territory," found in *Healing Song for the Inner Ear*. In my examination of these poems, I discuss Harper's literary explorations of aesthetics, memory, and geography as means for repairing misappropriations and distortions of the past. As such, "Acknowledgment" establishes a set of foundational frameworks for considering Harper's applications of the kinship mode in his poetic project.

At the same time, "Acknowledgment" also explores Harper's verse as developing a series of dialogues with "ancestral space." It recognizes the poet's engagement with family members and artists, along with specific works of art and geographic locations, as underscoring the extensive literary investigation of ancestry and kinship that Harper conducts throughout his body of work. It brings attention to the poet's efforts to establish kinship lines in his poetry and "acknowledge" a list of Black artists and cultural producers. In this way musicians, such as John Coltrane and Bessie Smith, and writers, like Ralph Ellison, Zora Neal Hurston, and Alice Walker, join members of Harper's immediate and extended family, including his paternal grandfather, Joseph Charles Harper, and son, Rolland Warren Harper, within the bonds of kinship.

In chapter 3, "Resolution (History as Mode)," the study considers the substantive engagement that Harper's poetry maintains with questions of history and issues of the past. Using the discussion of "generative kinship" as its foundation, in "Resolution" I examine the poet's well-defined sense of history and his distinct understanding of the past. In addition to recognizing Harper's "resolute" commitment to recovering elements of memory and matters from the past, the chapter addresses questions Harper raises about the construction of history throughout his poetic work. Several of Harper's early poems are discussed in this chapter, including "Song: I Want a Witness" and "American History," as well as individual pieces from the "Ruth's Blues" cycle ("Blue Ruth" and "History as Bandages") and the "Photographs/Negatives" sequence ("The Borning Room," "The Night of Frost," and "History as Apple Tree"). Drawing from critical works by Callahan and Stepto, "Resolution" brings additional perspectives to the historical dimensions of these poetic works.

In addition to examining works by these scholars, I draw on literary interviews with Harper by David Lloyd and John O'Brien to connect the term "convergent history" to the poet's poetic treatments of the past. In this way,

"Resolution" recognizes Harper's efforts to renew, revise, and even transcend the boundaries of received historical narratives, especially those that explore the color line in the United States, North American colonization, and the African diaspora. The chapter draws on a reading of familiar poems from Harper's first six volumes as well as "Archives," a poem found in the mid-career collection *Honorable Amendments,* which explores issues of the historical record through a set of observations that the poet makes during a visit to the American Baseball Hall of Fame and Library at Cooperstown, New York.

Chapter 4, "Pursuance (Black Music)," devotes attention to Harper's celebrated poetic explorations of Black music. Focusing on the poet's engagement with jazz figures and blues-rooted expression, I locate points of intersection where the music and its expressive traditions engage Harper's life experiences and literary project. In this chapter I draw on Harper's interview with John O'Brien and their conversation about the role jazz plays in the poet's body of work. To extend this discussion of Black music and the poet's verse, I also consider prose works by Harper, such as "Introducing the Blues" and "My Poetic Technique and the Humanization of the American Audience." Harper's insights and commentaries on Black music found in these works receive further clarification through a critical discussion by Anthony Walton and an interview with Reginald Martin. Ultimately, these discussions about jazz expand the analysis of two, frequently anthologized poems from *Dear John, Dear Coltrane,* "Alone" and "For Bud." These poems serve as a foundation for the discussion of Harper's poetic examination of blues-rooted expression and examination of "the mode" as the poet's principal device for framing his literary engagements with Black music. Thus, the chapter effectively underscores the intense artistic inquiry that Harper "pursues" throughout his poetic dialogue with the John Coltrane legacy.

Tracing engagements between the musician and the poet as they emerge throughout the course of Harper's career, a series of questions are explored in this chapter: What is jazz to Harper's poetry? How does it "become" or function within his body of work? Who is John Coltrane for the poet? These questions are addressed by analyzing the poet's engagements with Coltrane, jazz, and blues-rooted expression, drawing on a selection of Harper's later Coltrane poems from his final volume, *Use Trouble,* that includes the poems "A Coltrane Poem: September 23, 1998," "A Coltrane Poem: 9 23 99," and "The Book on Trane." "Pursuance" concludes with a discussion of "Dear John, Dear Coltrane," the titular work from the poet's first volume, after considering individual works from the "My Book on Trane" sequence, which appeared in *Healing Song for the Inner Ear.* With its reading of these lesser-known Coltrane poems—including "Sugarland," "Polls," and "Rumors"—Harper's body of work is connected to critical works by Herman Beavers, Kimberly W. Benston, and Gunter Lenz. Using essays by these scholars, along with interviews with Harper conducted by David Lloyd and Edward Hirsch, I explore "A Narrative of the Life and Times of John Coltrane: Played by Himself" and "Driving the Big Chrysler across the Country of My Birth." Through this line of inquiry, I examine Harper's literary engagements with the Coltrane legacy while locating points of intersection between "convergent history," "generative kinship," and "a love supreme" within his body of work.

The study concludes with chapter 5, "Psalm (Memory and Remembrances)." Extending the discussion of spirituality that emerges from Harper's literary engagements with Coltrane, jazz, and Black music, "Psalm" brings consideration to the poet's sustained concern for matters of memoria, death, dying, and memory. The chapter brings particular attention to Harper's adaptive work with the elegy as well as his interpretation of the praise poem, including "Double Elegy," "Use Trouble," "The Poet's Voice," and other poems from *Healing Song for the Inner Ear, Honorable Amendments,* and *Use Trouble.* The chapter chronicles Harper's efforts to collect and preserve the artistic legacies of several mid–twentieth-century modernists, including Robert Hayden, James Wright, Jacob Lawrence, and Gwendolyn Brooks. "Psalm" explores Harper's efforts to articulate and honor aesthetic connections linking his work to artists who impacted his development. The chapter treats verse drawn exclusively from Harper's later volumes and discusses memory, connection, and loss as foundational elements in his poetic project, without relying on examples from his first six volumes.

In "Psalm" Harper's elegies and praise poems are described as active literary tools, and they are discussed as complex instruments, integral to the processes of "remembrance" and "recollection." Commenting on the interplay between poetic form and literary function that informs this dynamic exchange, I argue that Harper and his verse reconcile notions of tradition with innovative practice. "Psalm" also locates the double-edged expressions of celebration and lament Harper invests throughout his body of work while delivering these literary commentaries on his artistic kin. The discussion draws on these sources: Heather Tresler's "Office Hours: A Memoir and an Interview with Michael S. Harper"; Alicia Ostriker's "Psalm and Anti-psalm: A Personal View"; Sharon Olds's "Notes on Gwendolyn Brooks"; and Jonathan Blunk's considerations of Harper's relationship with James Wright, "Elective Kinship: Improvisations on Portraiture in the Poetry of Michael S. Harper." These works help demonstrate Harper's efforts to bear witness to the accomplishments of his literary ancestors and to commune with their legacies. Harper's own short essays, "Every Shut Eye Ain't Asleep" and "An Integer is Just a Number," as well as his *Callaloo* interview with Charles Rowell, are relevant in this connection. I hope this chapter offers an understanding of Harper's poetry and its enduring engagement with memory, experience, and literary tradition.

While this project seeks to explore Harper's body of work comprehensively and inclusively, some omissions become readily evident. For example, several of the poet's longer works and several poems of critical interest are not discussed in this book. Some of these works were too long to fit within the limits of the volume; others were not particularly well suited for the "love supreme" structure used in this study. An example of one omission is the Faulkner-inspired long poem, "Love Letters: *The Caribou Hills, the Moose Range*," found in the third section of *Song: I Want a Witness*. Similarly, none of the three longer poetic sequences that comprise *Debridement*—"History as Cap'n Brown," "Heartblow," and "Debridement"—are discussed in this volume.

These three poems do not receive attention, in part due to their length and in part due to consideration that these works receive in *To Cut Is to Heal*, the critical companion to the restored edition of *Debridement* that Harper produced in 2000. *To Cut Is to Heal* includes essays by Herman Beavers and Allison Bundy and an interview with Harper conducted by the volume's editor Ben Lerner, all of which provide insight into these poems and the larger project that brought them into being. As such, Harper's longer *Debridement* poems are discussed with more attentive continuity in these contexts than they would have received within this study.

At the same time, adequately engaging the longer works from *Song: I Want a Witness* or *Debridement* requires a discussion of the "difficulty" associated with the poet's efforts to realize his original vision of publishing these two volumes as one collection. Prior to the publication of the restored edition of *Debridement*, Professor Harper addressed this topic in an interview I conducted with him. Responding to a question I asked about "History As Cap'n Brown," his treatment of John Brown's 1859 raid on the Federal Arsenal at Harper's Ferry, Harper stated, "When I wrote the poem, I envisioned a larger discourse on tributaries that Hayden had sketched out in *The Black Spear* sequence. After *Debridement* and *Song: I Want a Witness*, which I conceived originally as a single work, I lost confidence in my abilities to appropriate these complexities" (Antonucci 502).

In addition to the *Debridement* sequences, this study does not several other longer works other longer works Harper's "Uplift from a Dark Tower" sequence. Composed as a four-part suite, "Uplift" charts the convergence of multiple tropes, including history, kinship, music, and memory in the poet's consideration of the Yaddo artist retreat in Saratoga Springs, New York. Harper's poem situates Yaddo across time and space, tracing the movements of individuals associated with the property's history and the Trask family, who imagined their estate as a "place of rest and refreshment [for] authors, painters, sculptors, musicians, and other artists." The four distinct components that form "Uplift"—"The Battle of Saratoga (Springs) Revisited," "Dining from a Treed Condition, an Historical Survey," "The Founding Fathers in Philadelphia," and "Psychophotos of Hampton"—locates Yaddo as an intersection where the Trasks, their family associates, converge and commune with artists and figures from the past. For example, in the poem Harper conjures Booker T. Washington, Aaron Burr, Alexander Hamilton, and Benedict Arnold while identifying their connections to the lives of lesser-known, seldom-discussed individuals, like the fifteen nineteenth-century Indigenous youths—mostly Sioux men—who died as students at the Hampton Institute or Etienne, an African man, whom the Trasks employed as their servant at Yaddo and described as "a cannibal."

The poet delivers a sweeping examination of the origins of the United States as well as construction of family and race, framed within a literary discussion of a genocidal, colonizing drive for cultural dominance through assimilation. Elizabeth Dodd discusses this sequence and its various components in two essays, "The Great Rainbowed Swamp: History as Moral Ecology in the Poetry of Michael S. Harper" and "Complexity Begins Responsibility: Modernist Technique as Ethical Foundation in the Poetry of Michael S. Harper." Like the poetic sequences covered in To Cut Is to Heal, Dodd's essays serve as valuable points of entry for readers interested in accessing a critical conversation about the poet's longer works.

"Uplift" and the Debridement sequences are just two of Harper's longer poetic sequences and poetic cycles from this study also leaves untreated. Unfettered by spatial limitations, this volume would include a chapter on these poems as well as the poet's other longer works, such as "The Fret Cycle" from Use Trouble; his "Frederick Douglass Cycle" from Songlines in Michaeltree; and Harper's homage to collagist Romare Bearden, "Songline from a Tessera(e) Journal," found in Honorable Amendments. Each of these titles, along with the other lengthy works listed above, clearly qualify as "under-examined poems by Michael S. Harper" that this study seeks to explore. However, given spatial constraints they have not made their way into this discussion of the poet's explorations of jazz, history, and memory.

Finally, I do not discuss the elegies that Harper wrote to honor and grieve the passing of his two sons, Reuben Masai Harper and Michael Steven Harper Jr., who passed away shortly after their births, succumbing to acute respiratory distress syndrome. These deeply personal poems, including "We Assume: On the Death of Our Son, Reuben Maasai Harper"; "Reuben, Reuben";

"Deathwatch"; "The House on Miramar"; "Buck"; and "Nightmare Begins Responsibility," have been discussed over the years by numerous critics and scholars, such as Stepto and Callahan as well as Edwin Fussell. This set of poems and the conversations about them have informed Harper's reputation as a poet of family, connection, and kinship. In this way, I look "elsewhere" in its consideration the poet's explorations of family and kinship as "a love supreme."

CHAPTER 2

Acknowledgment (Kinship)

Michael S. Harper presents a set of observations about timing, plans, and improvisation in his autobiographical essay, "Every Shut Eye Ain't Asleep; Every Goodbye Ain't Gone." He offers the following account of the circumstances that led him to the University of Iowa in Robert Dana's *A Community of Writers: Paul Engle and the Iowa Writers' Workshop*: "I graduated from LA State College in winter 1961 and applied for a passport with intentions of going to Paris; I got a draft call to take my physical instead" (78). Acknowledging the sudden shift in his priorities, Harper writes that he decided "to get into graduate school immediately" (78). Having secured recommendations from a trio of Los Angeles State College English professors, including Christopher Isherwood along with Iowa Writers' Workshop alumni Henri Coulette and Wirt Williams, Harper submitted his application materials. He received an acceptance letter "with no fanfare and no financial aid, in mid-winter" (78).

The essay presents Harper's Iowa experience as the first steps on a path that would establish him among the distinct poetic voices of his generation. As such, this autobiographical literary collage becomes a source for examining the early stages of Harper's aesthetic and intellectual development. The essay amplifies points the poet makes in his mid-career autobiographical manifesto, "My Poetic Technique and the Humanization of the American Audience." In each of these meditations on his verse and writing process, Harper considers his experiences as a Black poet and the position he occupies within the American literary landscape. "My Poetic Technique" complements the effort Harper undertakes in "Every Shut Eye Ain't Asleep," exploring his body of work in terms of Black life, Black letters, and American experience, writ large.

Examining Harper's verse through this framework, his project is fully invested in the dynamic political, philosophical, and aesthetic transformations occurring within the United States as the Black Freedom Struggle's civil rights phase gave rise to the Black Power and Black Arts movements. As such, Harper's poetry works to contextualize Black experience in the United States. Throughout his eleven volumes of verse, published over a career spanning from the first Nixon administration to the presidency of Barack Obama, Harper delivers an annotated commentary on the "life and times" of the nation. Addressing questions of ancestry, lineage, and belonging throughout his body of work, Harper pursues a witnessing "witnessing" project, locating and probing the set of foundational identities—Black artist, family member, citizen of the United States, and so on—that he poet examines in his verse.

In "My Poetic Technique" Harper explores various identity categories—or modes—as he discusses his poetry's capacity to collect lore and establish connections. He offers an extended commentary on the impact that experience and perception make on the aesthetic and ethical sensibilities he engages in his verse. Working in this way, Harper proceeds to frame the ways that notions of kin and kinship function within his poetic project. Through the course of his essay, he discusses kinship modes that move beyond the limits of bloodlines and family trees. Harper regards kinship as a powerful means of connections within his verse that forges bonds between artists and writers that he understands as being every bit as strong as those linking parents to children and sisters to brothers.

Harper makes his case for these connections by drawing on the work of writers, musicians, and family members, whose presence and engagements within his poetry become sites and occasions for them to be recognized as "kin." The poet explores this impulse in "My Poetic Technique": "I have images of musicians at their best and when they were down and out; their playing never faltered; the other musicians wouldn't tolerate anything less . . . My people were good storytellers. Some of my personal kin walked north and west during the Civil War . . . I was surprised to find their images in books, not Stowe's *Uncle Tom's Cabin*, but Douglass' rhetoric, the notion of having each slave carry on his person an articulate pass, is my ticket to freedom" (30). With this gloss on his understanding of the intellectual, spiritual, and aesthetic dimensions of kinship, Harper presents his understanding of the concept as a fluid and evolving series of alignments rather than static units of "lineage."

Considered from this perspective "My Poetic Technique" responds to critical studies of Harper's early work by Robert B. Stepto and John F. Callahan that examine his verse through the lenses of "kin" and "kinship." For example, in "Michael S. Harper, Poet as Kinsman: The Family Sequences," Stepto reads Harper's first six volumes of poetry using kinship as the principal source of connection in these works. Callahan's treatment of Harper's verse published

between 1970 and 1977 similarly identifies kinship as the poet's principal conduit for accessing matters of experience, aesthetics, and identity. Callahan suggests that Harper's poetry exhibits "an extraordinary quality": his "poems of
kinship and tradition, [demonstrate] an intense energy that fuses rhetoric and
references with immediate experience" ("Testifying Voices in Michael Harper's
Images of Kin," 92).

Like Stepto and Callahan, Michael G. Cooke also explores Harper's poetry
through the dual lenses of kin and kinship. In *Afro-American Literature in the
Twentieth Century: The Achievement of Intimacy,* Cooke explains that Harper's work "virtually assigns itself to the category" of kinship, which the critic
defines as "a vision in growth and movement . . . where personal and commu-
nal powers surge together toward one goal" (40). Discussing Harper's "Song:
I Want a Witness" and "Alice," Cooke suggests that the poet's "collective and
personal approaches to kinship" expand limits and boundaries traditionally
associated with the category. In his exploration of Harper's "High Modes: Vision as Ritual: Confirmation," he describes the poem's engagement with kin
and kinship as being punctuated by a "*creative* metamorphosis" (120, emphasis
in original). Cooke goes on to align Harper's explorations of kinship with his
applications of "mode" and "modality."

In this way, Cooke delivers a commentary on Harper's interview with
Abraham Chapman interview with Harper, particularly where the poet offers
a working definition for his use of the terms "mode" and "modality." Asked to
explain how these concepts work within his poetic project, Harper states: "modality is irreducible . . . Modes are forces. [They] are always about relationship
. . . modality is also about energy" (Chapman, "An Interview with Michael S.
Harper," 465). Delivering a critique of Cartesian dualism and Western binary
thinking, Harper asserts that "modality is always about unity" (465). Seeking
clarification, Chapman summarizes the poet's position by stating: "if I understand you then, perhaps [it] is something like the ancient Chinese Taoist view
that everything has its own nature and everything is part of a universal order."
Harper responds: "A mode reveals its own truth on its own terms . . . What I'm
concerned about is the artistic arrangement of human essentials into the kind
of complement whereby certain qualities can be dramatized, certain attributes
can be connected to one another which do not in themselves seem to have relationships, which they in fact do have in a cosmic hierarchy" (466).

Harper's expansive sense of "the mode" moves toward the varied, flexible
idea of kinship that Cooke associates with Harper's verse. These connections become more evident as the poet continues his interview with Chapman
continues and he explains that "There is a responsibility and a connection
between my own technique and my own poetic traditions—what I come out

of and what is essentially an assortment of Black idioms and Black traditional motifs . . . [This pattern of development] has to do with American institutions . . . [and] how an individual comes to ascertain what is the province of one's thought and feeling and one's expression" (466). Sketching the parameters of his kinship mode in this way, Harper allows his poetry to map and locate its subject matter within and against an analytic grid that marks and measures identity and tradition.

Bringing discussions of Harper's early verse by Stepto, Callahan, Cooke, and Chapman into dialogue with one another, this study identifies "generative kinship" as a foundational component informing the poet's project. These critics' use of kin and kinship constructs conduits to engage Harper's verse, rather than creating applications for exclusionary sorting and sifting. As such, Harper's poetry presents possibilities for a modal kinship that advances "generatively," posing challenges to hard-and-fast lines of descent or unbending lineage. Through its use of generative kinship, Harper's verse creates links that subvert rigid, hierarchical notions concerning ancestry, family, and nation, which the poet regards as distorting the American psyche. He states in his interview with Chapman: "I think I have responsibilities to heroic traditions which are not connected with one's idiom, one's own ethnic province, but also with the larger concern of the American landscape, both In terms of its artistic achievement and its historical demands" (Chapman, "An Interview with Michael S. Harper," 466).

Pursuing these ends, Harper's poetry deploys generative kinship as an alternative to the disruptive displacement invested in the dynamics of kin as enacted through the exclusive binaries that inform American race ritual and race relations unfolding as they do against Jim Crow segregation and accompanying white supremacist tenets, including the "one drop rule," "scientific racism" and curtailed citizenship. Robert Stepto explores the generative possibilities of the kinship mode in "Michael S. Harper, Poet as Kinsman: The Family Sequences." Stepto acknowledges the impact of Harper's interview with Chapman in its epigraph. Drawing from this conversation, the critic quotes Harper as stating: "To speak about time and place and my own people as a kind of metaphor can be extended and applied to everybody, because I think everybody has a kind of kinship tie to everybody else" (477). Stepto discusses poems from *Dear John, Dear Coltrane, History Is Your Own Heartbeat, Song: I Want a Witness,* and *Nightmare Begins Responsibility,* tracing a set of varied and allusive connections that he recognizes as informing the generative kinship mode. He suggests that Harper's poetic project establishes the presence of "kin" within and about a range of figures and circumstances.

Stepto concludes his essay with a close reading of the poem "Grandfather." Presenting its forty-seven lines as a piece of "family lore," Stepto views
the poem as performing a set of literary interventions, at once enriching and
expanding the construction of Black experience and American history. "Grandfather" recalls events from the summer night in 1915 when a hostile white mob,
inspired by a screening of the film *Birth of a Nation,* gathered in front of the
Harper family residence in Catskill, New York. The poem's depiction of their
decision to attack one of the few Black families residing in that part of the
Hudson Valley presents white volatility and Black vulnerability as the enduring
tableaux of American experience. "Grandfather" gestures to a set of powerful
kinship bonds forged through family and cast in the crucible of racialized violence.

Through its depiction of the poet's paternal grandfather, Joseph Charles
Harper, the poem explores competing notions of kin and kinship that the
speaker sees informing the poem and American culture at large. On one
level, "Grandfather" presents the elder Harper as embodying the ideal of the
kinsman-protector, heroically prepared to defend home and family against a
volatile, threatening assembly. At the same time, however, the poem also poses
a set of profound questions concerning identity and belonging to Black people
in the United States. Stepto addresses this aspect of the poem in "Poet as Kinsman": "the scenario is absurd: Catskill, New York [becomes] the South" and "a
single black family [is] transmogrified into an entire race" ("Michael S. Harper:
Poet as Kinsman," 501). In this respect, anti-Black violence and American experience merge within the account.

An additional dimension of the "kinsman" ideal is appended to the poet's
discussion of his grandfather and the kinship mode. While Harper's kinsman
stands as a fierce defender and guardian, he also emerges from "Grandfather"
as a gentle and willing family servant, playful and caring, running footraces
with his grandson at the end of his workday. In Stepto's view, the poem effectively "transforms family lore into parable . . . [achieving an] obligatory
response to a kinsman's heroism in the face of recurring nightmare" (508).
Harper responds to Stepto in "My Poetic Technique and the Humanization of
the American Audience": "I wrote about my 'Grandfather' because he was a
hero in the highest sense, though he waited tables in white clothes. He taught
me to study Sugar Ray's left-hook technique, to step inside of someone's sense
of time . . . Ellison called it *antagonistic cooperation;* Wright called it the
switchblade of the movie screen. Language and rhetoric is essential power" (30,
emphasis in original). Recognizing the engagement "Grandfather" maintains
with the kinship mode, Harper explains that the poem presents his grandfather

as a modal and multivalent example of this concept in action. Recognizing the poem's capacity to enact "generative kinship" on multiple levels, Harper effectively connects life experiences to his poetic project as they unfold, on and off the page.

As this brief discussion of "Grandfather" illustrates, Harper imagines his poetry as both a means and occasion for connecting bloodlines and aesthetic models. The impulse toward fusing poetry and experience becomes evident as Harper links his paternal grandfather to the figure he depicts in his poem. He confirms that they are one and the same ("I wrote [the poem] about my 'Grandfather'"; 30). At the same time, through the coded, cross-referenced allusions that Harper makes to novelists Ralph Ellison and Richard Wright in his discussion of the poem, along with its reference to boxing legend Sugar Ray Robinson, he effectively understands "Grandfather" as a celebration of Black experience, Black expression, and Black identity.

Harper's vision of kinship expands an inclusive category of connection through both the poem and the essay. It welcomes the possibility that legacies and allegiances can be built upon actions and values, rather than on abstract and exclusive categories like race and blood. Harper's discussion of the poem and kinship from "My Poetic Technique" effectively supports the "kinship as art" reading of his project that Stepto delivers in "Poet as Kinsman." Identifying kin and kinship connections as he does, Stepto interprets "Grandfather" through the adage "Let the doing be the exercise, not the exhibition." Recalling that Harper borrowed this phrase from poet Sterling A. Brown,[1] the critic connects the poem to the saying. Examining the "exercise" Harper's speaker conducts as he explores the notion of generative kinship and the "doing" it enacts, this dynamic becomes evident in the final lines of "Grandfather":

> and I see cigar smoke in his eyes,
> chocolate Madison Square Garden chews
> he breaks on his set teeth,
> stitched up after cancer,
> the great white nation immovable
> as his weight wilts
> and he is on a porch
> that won't hold my arms,
> or the legs of the race run
> forwards, or on film
> played backwards on his grandson's eyes. (66)

Presenting kinship as a multidimensional mode, encompassing experience, identity, and family, these lines gesture to a transcendence of the category's conventional markers. Witnessing "the race run forward" and the "film played backward," the speaker of Harper's poem extends boundaries Black life and American identity. The poet constructs a vision for a nation and culture, locating points of entry for recollection and reflection, "on his grandson's eyes."

Walter Warren Harper, the poet's father, was an infant at the time of the attack on his family home that his son recounts in "Grandfather." Born June 29, 1915, the second of Florence Alexander and Joseph Charles Harper's five children, W. Warren Harper was reared and educated in Catskill, New York, a small town on the Hudson River, located about 125 miles north of New York City in Greene County. Warren worked for his father, whose diverse business ventures were conducted out of the newspaper and cigar shop he owned and operated near the town's ferry landing and New York Central Railway depot. Along with his brothers and sisters, Warren stocked and maintained "day line" boats that carried passengers to and from Catskill and New York City. While attending Catskill High School, Warren was the first Black-identified student to participate in varsity athletics, distinguishing himself as an excellent baseball and basketball player. His play on the court attracted the attention of the Syracuse University basketball program. However, unable to secure a full scholarship, Warren elected to enroll in the Civilian Conservation Corps (CCC) following graduation.

Assigned to a CCC camp in Williamsburg, Virginia, Warren confronted the codes and strictures of Southern-style segregation for the first time in his life. Having been raised in New York, the stark realities of Jim Crow were a focus of the letters he sent to his family. In his self -published memoir, I AM Katherine, the elder Harper recalls the disdain he felt upon being told by his CCC camp captain that "[Black] work crews [driving] to and from work . . . are not allowed to enter Williamsburg proper" (78). In addition to expressing misgivings about his experiences along the color line south of the Mason-Dixon, however, Warren's memoir also celebrates the sense of camaraderie he found among the other young Black men with whom he lived and worked while in the CCC. Recalling his time at the Williamsburg camp as "a good eight months" (80), he nevertheless elected to leave Virginia for New York City upon completing his term. As a result, it was only a short time after his arrival in New York he secured employment with a haberdasher and had the good fortune of encountering the woman who would become his wife and the mother of their three children.

Born on April 29, 1913, Katherine Louise Johnson—known as "Katti" within her family—was the second of Alice Braxton and Dr. Roland R. Johnson's three children. In I Am Katherine, Warren Harper describes Katti as having had a "relatively sheltered" upbringing, "confined" by the visibility that came with being one of "the Johnson children" (31). As the daughter of a Black physician and grandchild of African Methodist Episcopal Church Bishop John Albert Johnson, Katti and her two siblings were subject to the scrutiny of a tight-knit, Black middle-class community living in Brooklyn. In *I Am Katherine*, Warren explains that his wife was more comfortable playing marbles and mumblety-peg with her brother and other neighborhood boys. He describes her early years as being punctuated by "scuffed shoes and stockings torn at the knees" (33), which suggests that Katti resisted social expectations.

Seeking to instruct their daughter in "manners and social graces," Katti's parents enlisted the assistance of Edie Braxton Ford, her mother's eldest sister. Happily taking up the challenge, "Aunt Edie" regularly brought Katti and her sister into Manhattan for visits to museums, Central Park, and other sites of interest. According to Warren's memoir, spending time with her aunt soon became one of Katti's favorite things to do. Yet despite Aunt Edie's efforts, her niece maintained a passion for sports, especially football. This ultimately worked in Warren's favor in the fall of 1935 when he asked Katti if she would go with him to the Polo Grounds for a football game between the New York Giants and a team of college all-stars. Describing this first date as "a successful outing," the elder Harper suggests that this was one of many sporting events they would attend together in their fifty-plus year relationship.

The couple's connections continued to intensify as they enrolled for classes together at Brooklyn College in 1936. According to Warren Harper's memoir, their decision to do so represented a significant development. Although Katti had always been "a reluctant student," Warren was able to persuade her to attend classes with him. In *I Am Katherine*, he writes: "[The] closeness of surnames placed us in the same registration group, so we were able to work together. . . . We managed to get the same days and hours" (125). With Brooklyn College serving as their courtship's staging ground, Warren gained the Johnson family's approval by aligning himself with their strong belief in education.

Having won the admiration of his future in-laws, the couple began, in Warren's words, to "get serious." They wed on August 22, 1937, at St. John the Baptist Roman Catholic Church in Brooklyn. Immediately after, they moved into a duplex located at 816 Lafayette Avenue, just down the block from Katti's parents. The newlyweds shared this Brooklyn address with the bride's Aunt Edie and Uncle Jack Ford. In the spring of 1938, the couple welcomed the arrival of their first son, Michael; their second son, Jonathan Paul, in 1941; and their daughter, Katherine, in 1943.

Given Harper's poetic explorations of the kinship mode, the details of his parents' courtship and marriage assume a particular significance, especially in light of the numerous critical discussions that examine kinship's place within his poetic project. Works by Stepto, Callahan, Cooke, and others, including

Harper himself in "My Poetic Technique," bring attention to the poet's use of kinship in his verse, from *Dear John, Dear Coltrane* to *Use Trouble*. For example, Stepto's reading of "Grandfather" from "Poet as Kinsman" understands the poem as using the kinship mode as a way of engaging questions of identity and belonging. As such, "Grandfather" stands as an illustration of the poet's sense of kin as an assemblage comprising individuals who can be immediate family members—children, spouses, parents, siblings, and so on—but ultimately maintain particular experiential, aesthetic, and intellectual bonds. Harper constructs a family tree that sinks deep roots and spreads wide branches, which he animates through the image of "the well-knit family" (494). The dynamics of this kinship structure and its representation become fully evident in "Here Where Coltrane Is," the final piece of the twenty-poem "Ruth's Blues" cycle that Harper includes in *History Is Your Own Heartbeat*.

Celebrating the triumphs and acknowledging the complexities that Harper understands as integral to sustaining kinship, "Here Where Coltrane Is" demonstrates the poet's understanding of kin as a generative nexus, forged through function and process, rather than created by biology or nature. His sense of this assembly's capacity for development becomes evident in the opening lines of "Here Where Coltrane Is":

> Soul and race
> are private dominions,
> memories and modal
> songs, a tenor blossoming,
> which would paint suffering
> a clear color, but is not in
> this Victorian house
> without oil in zero degree
> weather and a forty-mile-an-hour wind;
> it is all a well-knit family:
> *a love supreme.* (32)

As the entry point for Harper's speaker and his engagement with the family –kinship–poetry assemblage, these opening lines capture the poet's sense of metaphor, conveying its imprint on his literary project. "Here Where Coltrane Is" becomes the poet's vehicle for exploring questions of memory, belonging, loss, and healing. Collecting these currents as "memories and modal/ songs," the poem's speaker identifies their power and presence in the "private dominions" that arrive as "soul and race" at the outset of the poem.

Similarly, through the mysterious and beautiful image of a "tenor blossoming," the poet establishes boundaries for a kinship mode that becomes defined,

familiar, and sustained in the image of the "well-knit family." According to
Robert Stepto, by locating these points of convergence as it does, the Ruth's
Blues cycle "investigates the process of kinship, including that aspect of kinship involving self-knowledge" ("Michael S. Harper, Poet as Kinsman," 483).
Examining Harper's sense of these connections as being "knit" or "sewn,"
Stepto presents the poet as creating a "kind of 'bandage,' healing memories of
loss and recurring nightmare" that effectively "tell us something of the poet's
role and responsibilities in creating kinship" (486). Read in this way, the "well-
knit family" that Harper presents over the course of "Ruth's Blues" manifests
in "Here Where Coltrane Is" as the space where his Brooklyn/Hudson Valley/
African roots contact the carpeted, midwestern whiteness of the Minnesota
prairie that he's come to share with his wife, children, and mother-in-law.

"Here Where Coltrane Is" reframes notions of kinship informed by American racial binaries, with the poet's family "blossoming" in a transcendent space
that is, at once, intergenerational and interracial. Acknowledging that he has
been propelled "here" by the power of Black music, Harper establishes the
poem's intersection with the chant from John Coltrane's four-part suite, *A Love
Supreme*.[2] The poem illustrates the impact of Coltrane's music on Harper's poetic project. In the final six lines of the poem's opening stanza, the poet initiates
a discussion of Coltrane's aesthetic and spiritual vision when he writes,

> I play "Alabama"
> on a warped record player
> skipping the scratches
> on your faces over the fibrous
> conical hairs of plastic
> under the wooden floors. (32)

Describing the listening act he performs as a recorded version of Coltrane's
"Alabama" plays on a turntable, the speaker establishes a powerful double
kinship bond, gesturing to the two kinship modes that he invests in the poem.

Harper is aware that this track from Coltrane's *Live at Birdland* album
stands as the musician's response to the September 15, 1963, bombing of the
16th Street Baptist Church in Birmingham, Alabama. As the record spins and
the music plays, the poet, along with the family members present with him in
the "Victorian house/ without oil," become enveloped in Coltrane's remembrances of Addie Mae Collins (14), Cynthia Wesley (14), Carole Robertson (14),
and Carol Denise McNair (11), the so-called "Four Little Girls" killed in the
blast. The poet's act of listening not only connects him to the murdered Black
children, but also allows him to "play" the music with Coltrane's Quartet.

By doing so, Harper's speaker effectively enacts a variation on the "kinship as art" notion that Stepto explores in "Poet as Kinsman." The poet feels and sees what Coltrane does, hearing "Alabama" and finding kinship in the music. At the same time, by engaging Coltrane's artistic vision in this way, Harper's speaker (a person of African descent living in the United States) also experiences what Stepto calls a "bloodline kinship" with Birmingham's Four Little Girls. In this way, doubling back through his own art, Harper extends both types of kinship connection to the members of the "well-knit family"—and their varying backgrounds—who experience the moment, "here where Coltrane is," with the poet.

Harper's speaker makes these connections while stationed at his listening post, "under wooden floors," stoically acknowledging the challenges facing his "well-knit family." However, he seems to suggest that being "without oil in zero degree weather/ and a forty-mile-an-hour wind" is part of the kinship building process that "blossoms" as "a love supreme." Understanding these circumstances as being transient, Harper instead expresses concern about the sonic distortions, obstructing the medium for Coltrane's music. Within the "Ruth's Blues" cycle, the "warped" turntable and "scratches" on the LP's "conical hairs of plastic" (32) become more of a threat to building kin and kinship than the wind and cold.

Commenting on the inability of contemporary sound recording and transmission dynamics to capture and convey Coltrane's musical message in this way, the poet delivers a critique of the historical record and the imperfections of the archive. As such, these inadequacies arrive as variations on Ralph Ellison's notions of "historical amnesia" and "the underground of unwritten history." At the same time, engaging these subjects from a subterranean space of retreat while listening to recorded jazz, Harper's speaker also contacts the protagonist in Ellison's *Invisible Man*. "Here Where Coltrane Is" contributes to an extended conversation concerned with the color line and American identity, generated by Black artists.

In the poem's second stanza, Harper's speaker continues examining the music, seeking out a space "where Coltrane is." Moving deeper into the musician's work, his exploration of the possibilities it generates for representing "kinship *as* art" expands. Embracing the power of what might be termed "aesthetic kinship" in this way, the poet ultimately locates himself and his family within a broader "kinship *of* art." As such, "Here Where Coltrane Is" identifies a transcendent realm where the power of everyday influences—substandard stereo equipment, oil deliveries, and weather reports—diminish. The poet signals his arrival in this space:

> Dreaming on a train from New York
> to Philly, you hand out six
> notes which become an anthem
> To our memories of you:
> oak, birch, maple,
> apple, cocoa, rubber.
> For this reason Martin is dead;
> for this reason Malcolm is dead;
> for this reason Coltrane is dead;
> in the eyes of my first son are the browns
> of these men and their music. (33)

With these lines, the poem's speaker experiences a shift in his relationship to Coltrane and his musical legacy. Having entered the music as an active listener, the poet becomes an engaged interlocuter, contacting the musician "on a train from New York/ to Philly." Accessing this space—"where Coltrane is"—the boundaries of both their conversation and identities as artists, as Black men, and as kin expand. Understanding what it is to "play 'Alabama,'" the poet and Coltrane establish their kinship bonds, at once, both as and through their art.

This transition becomes evident as Harper's speaker hears the musician "hand out six / notes which become an anthem."[3] The music delivers an invitation to move further into this expressive realm, which the poet ultimately accepts. Transported by his listening act, Harper's speaker locates his family's varied points of intersection with and along the American color line. Surveying the stark realities of this space, acknowledging its capacity for storing pain and loss, Harper's speaker records the need to repair damages enacted upon people of African descent from the time of their arrival in the Western hemisphere to the present day.

To begin this process, the poet lists six types of trees: "oak, birch, maple, / apple, cocoa, rubber." Resonating with the cadence of the six-note anthem Coltrane "hands out" in "Alabama," the list establishes a line of connection between these trees and the New World African experience. In this way, "Here Where Coltrane Is" notes the sonic force and intensity of Coltrane's composition while delivering a gloss on imperial conquest and resource extraction in the Americas. Harper's poem acknowledges the imprint that colonialism, racism, disease, and targeted violence has made on Black experience. The harsh realities of slavery, plantation labor, and lynching reverberate through the poet's trees, striking their limbs and trunks, settling in their roots, and ultimately identifying another layer of kinship "where Coltrane is."

Establishing these bonds, grounded in what may be understood as "cultural kinship," Harper ultimately links his poetic project to Coltrane's musical legacy. According to Stepto, poet and musician both exhibit a common commitment to realizing "the artist's obligations to traditions and for living a life morally and well" (487). Continuing to identify kinship mode connections between Coltrane's "Alabama" and "Here Where Coltrane Is," the critic presents these two works as illustrating "a few of the infinite dimensions of moral conscience transformed into tonal metaphor" (487). As such, Harper's poem merges "bloodline kinship" with "kinship as art," joining Coltrane's attempt to "bandage" the wounds of a nation, injured and broken by its harsh realities and brutal truths. These connections between blood and aesthetics are reenforced as "Here Where Coltrane Is" concludes, with the poet at once acknowledging the power of loss—citing the deaths of Malcolm X, Dr. Martin Luther King Jr., and John Coltrane—while celebrating the redemptive possibilities of Black expression. This impulse becomes evident in the final two lines of "Here Where Coltrane Is," as the legacies of these three twentieth-century Black cultural figures—"the browns/ of these three men"—enter "the eyes" of the poet's "first son."

Continuing to examine Harper's explorations of bloodlines and songlines,[4] Stepto suggests that the poet engages "the artist's role as redeemer." The critic sees him carry out this project by working with the "kinship portrait." In "Poet as Kinsman," he identifies the poet's use of this distinct type of kinship poem as a means to (a) process circumstances and situations that exist beyond his immediate range of experience or (b) treat figures and concepts outside the limits of family. In this way, Harper's kinship portraits function by connecting the poet and his work to lives and experiences away from the "well-knit family" (unlike "Here Where Coltrane Is" or "Grandfather"). For Stepto, Harper's treatment of blues singer Bessie Smith in "Last Affair: Bessie's Blues Song," a poem from the *Song: I Want A Witness* collection, stands as a prime example of this type of exploration of the kinship mode.

In the opening stanza of "Last Affair," Harper's speaker constructs a portrait of Bessie Smith, identifying the imprint that the Empress of the Blues makes upon both Black America and American popular music. Through the course of the poem, the poet links Bessie and her music to his work with cultural kinship. He begins by establishing these connections:

> Disarticulated
> arm torn out,
> large veins cross
> her shoulder intact,

> her tourniquet
> her blood in all-white big bands (63)

Tracing bonds of "blood" and "aesthetics," Harper explores cultural flows along and across the American color line. Through its account of the blues singer's career and the circumstances of her death, "Last Affair" examines race relations and race rituals, as the poet does in "Here Where Coltrane Is." Like the well-knit family, Bessie's "tourniquet" becomes a bandage for the wounds of segregation and denial. The stanza's stoic account of this dynamic concludes as the poet identifies the singer's "blood in all-white big bands."

Executing a shift as the poem continues, Harper's speaker moves from this factual reportage to a series of six-line stanzas. Delivering a combination of open and closed rhymes—"Mississippi road"/ . . . her ham bone" ; "her neck/ . . . black train wreck/ . . . same stacked deck"—the poet invests "Last Affair" with a sense of blues vernacular. In an alternate version of the poem, Harper's pursuit of this sensibility becomes enhanced[5] as he incorporates an italicized chorus, presumably "sung" by Bessie Smith, into the piece:

> *Can't you see*
> *what love and heartache's done to me*
> *I'm not the same as I used to be*
> *this is my last affair* (63)

Over the course of the poem, these blues are repeated as Harper's speaker renders his portrait of the singer. As their voices interweave and form a single vision, "Last Affair" surveys the empire of Bessie's songs, mapping both Black America and the nation as a whole. Harper's poem gestures toward the possibility of a cultural transformation where, according to Stepto, "kinship is ripe and the interior landscape is better known" (492).

"Poet as Kinsman" appeared in the *Massachusetts Review* shortly after the publication of *Nightmare Begins Responsibility*. The essay effectively functions as a review of that collection, while summarizing the initial phase of the poet's career. As such, Stepto's piece offers insight about the foundation of Harper's literary project. The critic's work also provides contemporary readers with a valuable snapshot of how the poet's "most recent collection of verse" was received when it was published. At the same time, "Poet as Kinsman" also illustrates how the kinship portrait developed into a hallmark of Harper's body of work. As the essay carries out these projects, it focuses on poems from "Kin" and "Nightmare Begins Responsibility," two of the five sections that comprise the *Nightmare Begins Responsibility* volume.

However, despite the attention "Poet as Kinsman" brings to this collection, the critic's essay does not discuss any of the thirteen poems found in the "Sterling Letters" section of *Nightmare Begins Responsibility*. The poems in this volume's fifth and final section (which largely remain underexamined) map the poet's "extended family tree" and illustrate his inclusive approach to terms like "kinship," "culture," and "artist." These impulses are seen, for example, in the five pieces from "Sterling Letters" that Harper dedicates to poet Sterling A. Brown and his spouse, Daisy. They also become evident in poems he writes for other Black writers, such as "Gains" (for Ernest J. Gaines), "Corrected Review: THEREISATREEMOREANCIENTTHANEDEN" (for Leon Forrest), and "Paul Laurence Dunbar: 1872–1906" (for Paul Laurence Dunbar). Along with these poems, the poet includes works in this section of *Nightmare Begins Responsibility* dedicated to nonliterary Black cultural figures, such as baseball great Willie Mays and legendary gospel singer Mahalia Jackson.

Considering various branches of the poet's family tree, the "Sterling Letters" section of *Nightmare Begins Responsibility* arrives at its conclusion with "Alice," a poem that Harper dedicates to poet and novelist Alice Walker. As the final poem of the volume's closing section, "Alice" literally and figuratively delivers this collection's last word. The poet's decision to assign this duty to the poem becomes significant, recalling that Alice Walker had yet to become a household name. At the time of the volume's publication, Walker's essay "Looking for Zora" had only recently found its way to the pages of *Ms.* magazine and neither her Pulitzer Prize-winning novel, *The Color Purple,* nor her groundbreaking essay collection, *In Search of Our Mothers' Gardens*, had been published.

In addition to delivering its account of Walker's successful search for the unmarked burial site of Zora Neale Hurston, "Alice" and "Last Affair: Bessie's Blues Song," are prime examples of Harper's engagement with "kinship portraiture." With its two distinct cantos, "Alice" simultaneously praises, summarizes, and contextualizes Walker's successful efforts to locate and recover Hurston's literary and intellectual legacy. In "Alice," Harper conveys his understanding of Walker's work as establishing both blood and aesthetic kinship bonds with Hurston.[6] These two distinct kinship modes are present in the poem's first stanza, where Harper's speaker delivers his account of Walker's search for the "novelist, folklorist and anthropologist":

> You stand waist-high in snakes
> beating the weeds for the gravebed
> a quarter mile from the nearest
> relative, an open field in Florida: lost,

> looking for Zora, and when she speaks
> from her sunken chamber to call
> you to her side she calls
> you her distant cousin, her sister
> come to mark her burial place
> with a bright black stone. (96)

As Harper's speaker transports himself to "an open field in Florida" during the summer of 1973, he witnesses the blues-rooted, call-and-response exchange between the two Black women writers during their initial encounter with each other. By capturing this moment as he does, the poet delivers his account of Hurston and Walker's "family reunion" in the Garden of Heavenly Rest Cemetery, effectively portraying both women as participants in a collaborative, recovery effort.

Establishing their kinship connections, the poet acknowledges the writers as having overcome a list of obstacles, including weeds, snakes, and death. "Alice" posits that Hurston and Walker are bound within a network of bloodlines and aesthetic connections. Recognizing the strength of these writers' bonds, the poet observes them renaming and reimagining one another. Locating and identifying their sources of connection, the women exchange the titles "distant cousin" and "sister." The speaker congratulates Walker for solving the departed writer's "conjure-riddle" by locating her "sunken chamber" as the poem continues. Addressing Walker before the opening stanza concludes, the poet confidently asserts that Hurston—"lost" in her "grave bed" for thirteen years—"has known you would do this." Paraphrasing Hurston, he presents *her crooked stick, her straight lick* as tools, ready-made, for assisting Walker as she goes about "calling her to communion" (96, emphasis in original).

The poet continues to develop his portrait of Walker and Hurston, accounting for their kinship bonds in the second stanza of the poem's first canto. Shifting his focus from the writers' initial encounter, the speaker observes the two women's sense of growing connection. He identifies a set of aesthetic intersections that Hurston and Walker share with each other:

> you have paid your homage
> in traditional line, the face open:
> your face in the woman-light of surrender
> toughened in what you were. (96)

Once again addressing Walker directly, the poet witnesses the sustained engagement she maintains with Hurston. Unfolding their mutual investment in Black expression, the speaker frames the writers' interactions evoking "tradition" and belonging. The poet probes the aesthetic foundations of Hurston and Walker's kinship bonds. Citing "ancestral space" and "a black rock of ages," he locates shared boundary sites that link the two Black writers' and their literary projects.

Harper expands his poetic excavation project as "Alice" moves into its second canto. Tracing the elements that shape and sustain their exchange, the poet presents Hurston and Walker as partners in a larger, shared undertaking. Supporting his sense of these connections, he selects images and moments from their respective bodies of work, including Hurston's *Their Eyes Were Watching God* and Walker's short story "The Garden." The speaker identifies both writers as incorporating the landscape of the southern United States into their work, presenting the South as being both "home" and a treacherous, even deadly environment for Black people. Harper's poetic portrait of these writers invests their work into a broader discussion of cultural kinship. As such, he presents the two women contributing to an extended survival project that stands "for centuries of motherhood and atonement / for which you write, and the rite written" (97).

As canto two's second stanza begins, the speaker abruptly adjusts his approach to discussing Walker, Hurston, and their kinship mode. Abandoning the detailed, artist-to-artist conversational portraiture he employs in the first three stanzas of "Alice," the poet shifts to personal narration, describing his own visit to Hurston's burial site. Situating himself within the Garden of Heavenly Rest cemetery, paying homage to both Hurston and Walker, the poem's speaker aligns himself and his family with these women's extended literary discussion of kinship and continuity in Black culture. He initiates this process, engaging their shared legacy: "And for this I say your name: Alice, / my grandmother's name, your name"[7] (97).

Gesturing to a set of common connections, rooted in a transitive reading of both blood and aesthetic kinship, the poet constructs a lineage, linking himself to Walker's efforts to locate and mark Hurston's burial site. Creating another type of "well-knit family," the poet once again tends to wounds created by segregation, racial division, and social inequities. Merging kinship, culture, and remembrance, Harper expands the limits of these connections when he writes,

> and where I speak from now
> on higher ground of her risen
> black marker where you have written
> your name in hers, and in mine. (97)

"Alice" concludes as the poet grafts new branches onto his family tree. Making his observations from the Fort Pierce, Florida burial ground where Walker reclaimed Hurston's legacy, Harper's speaker identifies this "open field in Florida" as a kinship nexus, rooted in the expressive traditions that inform these Black writers and their work.

The poet presents the kinship mode as his means to examine the dynamics of connection, belonging, and memory, along with moments of healing and loss. Harper's poetic project acknowledges these elements as forming and informing his engagements with various types of kinship. In poems such as "Alice" and "Grandfather," these experiential components converge, charting the family–kinship–poetry flows Harper logs throughout his body of work. At the same time, these kinship portraits also locate the geographic dimensions that form the foundations of Harper's verse. For example, in "Alice," the poet documents site-specific acts of reconciliation and recovery. Hurston's "sunken chamber" and the cultural landscape of the American South arrive as poetic features, establishing the poem's sense of place and spatial identity.

Like Harper's other kinship poems, "Alice" surveys sites where cultural features—such as family, race, history, and nation—converge, forging kinship bonds, situated in region and oriented by geography. The poem thus provides the poet with an opportunity to explore the kinship mode, bringing particular attention to details that relate to location. By engaging specific cultural features and geographic elements, Harper's kinship portraits contextualize the contours and configuration of these sites. This dynamic occurs throughout Harper's body of work. Whether he's sketching events in New York's Hudson Valley, the "Victorian House without heat," or a Florida cemetery, geography functions as both source and resource within his literary survey of the American cultural landscape.

Mapping cultural space as he does, the poet simultaneously connects portions of Black America to American experience, more broadly defined while working to create distinctions between the two. Harper's poetic project records and makes reference to what Ralph Ellison calls the "territory." The poet understands this region as an assemblage of features and sites, possessing the capacity to witness, collect, and archive Black experience, both generally and individually. Harper's verse effectively serves as a repository for events, incidents, and occasions that escape the notice of American consensus historiography.

Maintaining this particular relationship with "the territory," Harper's kinship portraits inform the poet's critique of American history. His spatially oriented literary project links lived experience and family lore to broader notions of American culture, effectively enhancing the visibility of what Ellison describes as "the American underground of unwritten history" ("Going to the 'Territory'" 126). Harper traces boundary lines and crosses border lands, creating a catalog of voices, sounds, and actions and outlining the enclaves and districts that construct Black America. Drawing from a broad range of geographical referents—churches, concert halls, athletic arenas, libraries, and juke joints—Harper's body of work speaks back to a variety of sources that includes archival documents, recorded music, and photographs, by engaging the ebb and flow of the Black vernacular, using what the poet calls "the grapevine."

Working in this way, Harper's poetic exploration of American cultural geography effectively invites the territory to speak. In the lengthy epigraph he includes with "My Poetic Technique and the Humanization of the American Audience," Harper alludes to the "geo-poetic" impulses that inform his literary project. He quotes novelist Ralph Ellison, who states: "The geographical division of the country into political districts and regions with complementary agricultural and economic systems underlies much of Afro-American poetic symbolism. That the star points north is not important because of abstract, or mystical or religious conception . . . [it is rooted in] the fact that if you got safely across certain socio-geographical boundaries you were in freedom" (Harper and Stepto, *Chant of Saints*, 27). Ellison's consideration of space, place, and freedom serves as the foundation for the poetic manifesto and autobiographical study that the poet delivers in "My Poetic Technique." Ellison's explanation of the relationship between geography and Black America informs this piece and its exploration of the kinship mode.

These links become evident as the poet conducts his geo-poetic mapping exercise, surveying individuated, interior spaces (such as his parents' record collection), and sites of collective exchange, like classrooms, alleyways, the New York City subway system, and blues-rooted music. These locations punctuate a list of urban landscapes where he makes these observations, which includes Brooklyn, Manhattan, Los Angeles, and Johannesburg. To further underscore the connections he sees linking geography and the kinship mode, Harper writes: "My people were good storytellers. Some of my personal kin walked north and west during the Civil War from North Carolina, South Carolina, and Virginia, and one ancestor came from Chatham—Ontario, Canada. I was surprised to find their images in books, not Stowe's *Uncle Tom's Cabin*" (Harper, "My Poetic Technique" 30). Offering this first-person commentary on his family history, space, and Black life, the poet effectively issues a point-by-point response to Ellison's call for writers and scholars to acknowledge geography's relationship to Black experience in the United States.

Ellison would go on to refine his thoughts about space, place, and Black life in the United States, ultimately incorporating them into "Going to the Territory," the keynote address he delivered at the Ralph Ellison Festival held at Brown University in 1979.[8] The text of this talk would become the title piece for

Going to the Territory, the final collection writing that Ellison published in his lifetime. In this essay, the novelist suggests that Black expression is created and enacted within an interlocking, spatialized kinship network: "it is no accident that so much of the symbolism of [Black] folklore is rooted in the imagery of geography" (131).

The novelist makes a case that throughout the eighteenth and nineteenth centuries, enslaved and newly liberated people of African descent living in the United States were keenly aware of space, place, and environment. Paraphrasing the pre-Socratic Greek philosopher Heraclitus, Ellison plainly states that in Black America, "geography was fate" (131). To support his claim, he references the lyrics of Bessie Smith's "Workhouse Blues." Presenting the song as evidence of the prominent place geography occupies within Black experience, Ellison understands Smith's recording as capturing geo-cultural realities that he witnessed as a Black youth, coming of age in Oklahoma City, Oklahoma. He explains that in addition to looking North, Black Americans understood that "freedom was also to be found in the West of the old Indian Territory," writing that "Bessie Smith gave voice to this knowledge when she sang of 'Going to the Nation, Going to the Terr'tor'" (131). Ellison's essay forges a set of kinship bonds linking Bessie's blues to his literary project.

Harper delivers a poetic coda on Ellison's discussion of the aesthetic kinship bonds the novelist establishes between himself and Bessie Smith in a poem entitled "Goin' to the Territory." This thirty-one-line piece arrives in *Healing Song for the Inner Ear,* along with two companion poems, "The Body Polity" and "The Pen," as the final work in the poet's three-part sketch of Ellison, his novel, and their literary legacy. Although none of the three poems are explicitly dedicated to the novelist, images and titles used in this poetic triptych both reference and reflect specific aspects of Ellison's life and work. Through the course of the call-response dialogue these poems enact, the poet and the novelist address a set of shared concerns about geography and Black life in the United States. As such, the poem amplifies a detailed exchange regarding kinship, the blues, Black letters, and geography. At the same time, "Goin' to the Territory" considers events, issues, and phenomena that the novelist observed and experienced with his mother and younger brother in the segregated Oklahoma City neighborhood known as "Deep Second," during the opening decades of the twentieth century.

In addition to presenting Ellison as a consummate Black literary artist, Harper's poem registers the imprint of Jim Crow segregation and its legacies on the geography of American culture. As such, "Goin' to the Territory" bundles material and information the poet collects from Ellison's "American underground of unwritten history." The poem gestures to possibilities that the novelist locates within "the territory." Surveying this space, as it does, "Goin' to the Territory" maps features of the territory while envisioning a means for subverting the limits and strictures of American white supremacy. Carrying out this double-edged project—effectively offering its own set of variations on the "twoness" of Du Boisian double consciousness—Harper's poem simultaneously enters and defines this environment. These dynamics become evident in the poem's first stanza when Harper's speaker states,

> *Ethical schizophrenia* you call it:
> come back to haunt the cattle-drive,
> Indians coming into blacktown
> because it's home; your father's will
> lies uncontested, his blood welling up in oil;
> "Deep Second" hones its marks on Jimmy Rushing;
> Charlie Christian's father leads the blind. (63)

Evoking *"ethical schizophrenia,"* as he does in these lines, the poet cites Ellison's term for the applied use of myth in depictions of American history and identity. Beginning his exploration of the territory in this way, Harper's speaker frames his discussion of the novelist within a kaleidoscopic vision of Black experience and its relationship to the development of American culture. Over the course of the poem's five stanzas, building upon a doubled and redoubled sense of these shifts and movements, the poet indexes a set of cultural and geographic features.

"Goin' to the Territory" draws from Ellison's impressions of his youth in the Old Southwest to frame a discussion of Black life during the early decades of the twentieth century. Tracing these kinship pathways throughout the course of his poem, Harper's speaker draws images and events from the novelist's accounts of his experiences in "the territory." The poem effectively identifies foundational components of Ellison's aesthetic sensibilities. Acknowledging the novelist's expansive sense of Black culture, examining the complex relationships that he explores in his "Going to the Territory" essay, the poem connects ranch hands to jazz musicians. As such, Harper's "Goin' to the Territory" effectively charts Ellison's understanding of shifting "norm(s) on the frontiers of American society" (134).

Building upon the "incongruous juxtapositions" that the novelist discusses in his essay by the same title, the poet presents an extended commentary on Black culture and aesthetics. For example, recognizing the power of improvisation upon and within Black experience, Harper's poem delivers an extended riff on questions relating to identity and place that Ellison treats throughout his fiction and non-fiction, alike. The complex cultural layering that the poet locates within the territory becomes evident in the poem when he offers the image of Indigenous stockyard workers—essentially "passing" as cowboys—returning to their living quarters in a segregated Black neighborhood. As such, the poet identifies an all-American set of incongruous kinship ties in the line "Indians coming into blacktown / because it's home." In this way Harper's speaker works to revise the unspoken and unquestioned assumptions by which white supremacy and "scientific" racism dictate terms along the color line. "Goin' to the Territory" aligns the "disruptive" impulses that the poet invests throughout its opening stanza. For example, drilling deep, Harper's speaker sees "blood welling up in oil" as he calls forth the legacies of Oklahoma City–born Black musicians Jimmy Rushing and Charlie Christian—whom Ellison wrote about in his essay collection, *Shadow and Act*. In this way, the poet acknowledges the novelist's connection to the blues roots of the Deep Second neighborhood.

Bending, breaking, and (ultimately) embracing the aesthetic and geographical kinship bonds he examines with his poem, Harper's speaker effectively doubles down on his exploration of the kinship mode. Investing Black lives and Black experience into the American West as it does, "Goin' to the Territory" works to claim space for Black America within a larger, broader American experience. Harper's poem brings attention to the geographic and cultural kinship ties that Ellison maintains with Rushing, Christian, and their music. Establishing links between vernacular expression and Black life, lived in "the territory" during the early twentieth century, the poet riffs on Oklahoman Woody Guthrie's geo-poetic folk anthem, "This Land Is Your Land." He does so, amplifying connections between space, place, and Black culture in the second stanza of "Goin' to the Territory," in his consideration of music by performed and composed by jazz greats Edward Kennedy "Duke" Ellington and Louis "Satchmo" Armstrong:

> Such instruments arrange themselves
> at Gettysburg, at Chickamauga;
> the whites in Tulsa apologize
> in the separate library,
> all the books you dreamed of,
> fairy tales and Satchmo jesting
> to the Court of St. James,
> infirmary is the saints already home. (63)

Once again, the poet connects specific elements of Black expression to Ellison's "underground of American unwritten history." Interweaving references to jazz, Jim Crow, the Tulsa Massacre, and Civil War battles, these lines position Armstrong and his music—each maintaining its own significance within

Ellison's novel—among a constellation of images the poet associates with "the territory." These sites converge in the poem's second stanza within a literary collage that incorporates history, geography, law, and imagination into an impressionistic exploration of Ellison, his work, and Black America.

Harper continues his exploration of geography and aesthetic kinship in the third stanza of "Goin' to the Territory." Treating the historical contexts and living conditions he understands as informing Black expression, the poet returns to his discussion of Ralph Ellison's lived experience and artistic legacy. Bringing the novelist into conversation with Duke Ellington, he writes:

> in documents, in acts won out
> on hallelujahs of "A" train,
> nine Scottsboro Boys spun upward
> over thresholds of Duke's dance. (63)

Presenting the two artists and their legacies entwined in a chain of kinship bonds, the speaker alludes to Ellington's composition "Take the 'A' Train." He recalls Harlem and New York of the 1930s and '40s, where Ellison, through his novel and its protagonist, made his observations on American race ritual and race relations. The poet extends his project, referencing the Scottsboro Nine, the group of Black youths—ranging in age from thirteen- to twenty-years old—falsely accused of rape by two white women from Alabama in 1931. The arrest, trials, and convictions of the nine youths, often referred to as "the Scottsboro Boys," were on Ellison's mind when he left Oklahoma City in a boxcar bound for Alabama to study music at Tuskegee in 1933.

With these sites and spaces informing the poem's account of Black experience, "Goin' to the Territory" presents Black artists like Armstrong and Ellington as making Black life more discernable upon and within the American cultural landscape. Identifying points of intersection and tracing kinship flows, this dynamic plays out on multiple levels throughout Harper's poem. The poet effectively joins Ellison in acknowledging Black expression—especially Black music—as delivering "humanized" response to the violence and trauma experienced throughout Black America. Both Harper and the novelist praise Black artists for marking boundaries of "the territory" and mapping the American color line. Harper's speaker extends these efforts in the fourth stanza of "Goin' to the Territory":

> Dance and mask collect their greasepaint,
> idioms stand on bandstand, in stove-
> pipe pants of a riverman, in gambling shoes,
> his gold-toothed venom vexing sundown,

the choir at sunrise-service cleansing
a life on a jim crow funeral car. (63)

The poet assembles a set of images drawn from the American minstrel tradition. Greasepaint, masks, gold teeth, dance, and stovepipe pants bring the poet into dialogue with powerful, ambiguous, double-edged possibilities rooted in "the idiom." Harper's speaker engages these nether regions of the territory through his minstrel figure of "the riverman."

Fully animated, extending stereotyped, two-dimensional limits of Black life's "pathos and humor," the riverman arrives, fingering "the jagged edge" of his own complexity.[9] Connecting himself to "possibilities" and "juxtapositions" that Ellison identifies with the territory and blues-rooted expression, Harper's speaker addresses the region's uncertain, shifting terrain through his minstrel figure. So often maligned and even villainized, the "riverman" receives a sense of purpose, if not a measure of dignity, as the poet allows him to "stand on bandstand" (63). Establishing himself within the continuum of Black culture, Harper's riverman figure emerges from the territory as the poet's kinsman, along with Ellison, Ellington, Bessie Smith, Coltrane, and others.

"Goin' to the Territory" concludes in the unrhymed couplet that becomes the poem's fifth stanza, where Harper's speaker proclaims, "The first true phrase sings out in barnyard; / the hunt in books for quail" (63). While these enigmatic lines return the poem's focus to Ellison and his Oklahoma roots, read as commentary concerned with the riverman's appearance "on a jim crow funeral car," the couplet signals this figure's timely arrival in a camouflaged refuge or a space of sanctuary. Like the protagonist from Ellison's *Invisible Man,* the riverman pursues an "invisibility / briar-patch" strategy, effectively hiding in plain sight. "Goin' to the Territory" speaks to the aesthetic and cultural kinship connections linking Ellison's project to the poet and his body of work through the Zen koan he embeds in these lines.

Harper's poem presents its own variation on what the novelist describes as his work's attempt to "rediscover the more obscure connections, through which the past has become a part of the living present" (Ellison, "Going to the Territory, 123). As writers and kinsmen, Ellison and Harper disrupt cultural expression that is "selective in [its] memory as well as in [its] priorities. . . . ignoring such matters as the shar[ed] bloodlines and cultural traditions by groups of widely differing ethnic origins, and by overlooking the blending and metamorphosis of cultural forms which is so characteristic of our society, [Americans] misconceive our cultural identity" (Ellison, "Going to the Territory," 125).

Harper ultimately articulates his commitment to this approach to kinship in the conclusion of "My Poetic Technique and the Humanization of the

American Audience." Addressing matters of "bloodlines and cultural traditions" in this autobiographical piece, the poet recalls his conversation with the Black South African courtesy van driver who transported him to his lodging upon his arrival in apartheid-era Johannesburg during a 1977 literary exchange. Adhering to rituals of apartheid, the driver attended to a group of white passengers first, asking Harper to wait behind at the airline terminal. When he returned, the poet writes that the driver "apologized for not taking me in the van with the other passengers. He wanted to know where I came from and then he asked—'What language do you speak when the White [*sic*] people aren't around?'" (32). Dissatisfied by Harper's initial response of "English," the poet continues by writing that the van driver said "'No, no.' [asking again] 'What language did I speak when White [*sic*] people weren't around?' The second time I changed my response to 'American.' 'Brother,' he inquired, 'when Blacks are among themselves, don't they speak jazz?' I nodded, *right on, brother*" (32).

Concluding "My Poetic Technique" with this travel sketch, Harper confirms the investment his poetic project makes in the kinship mode and blues-rooted expression. Through their exchange, poet and driver acknowledge that kinship's transformative power extends beyond the limits of ancestry, bloodlines, and family trees. They understand Black expression as connecting a varied array of cultural sites and spaces. These Black men effectively recognize this capacity as being articulated in the aesthetic practices and formal pursuits presented as "jazz." Acknowledging these kinship bonds, they become "a love supreme."

CHAPTER 3

Resolution (History as Mode)

> The real reason history is important is because life is
> tragic and American life is particularly tragic because so
> many possibilities exist and there's been so much waste.

> —Michael S. Harper

Harper undertakes a set of ambitious projects through his body of poetic work. Considering Black experience in the United States, he aims to bind fissures, bridge gaps, and heal wounds across a range of identity categories, including family, nation, and race. To do so, the poet explores expressive possibilities that emerge from his poetry's engagement with "the kinship mode." John F. Callahan identifies this impulse in his review of Harper's *Images of Kin*; he writes that the poet "is interested in lines of ancestry and kinship, ties made visible by blood and heredity and those other ties that manifest, but less visible, ties formed by that shared experience of American life" ("Testifying Voice," 90).

Callahan describes the new and collected poems found in this volume as Harper's "best and most representative work" ("Testifying Voice," 90). Considering the range of aesthetic, cultural, and ethical questions Harper addresses with the poems he includes in *Images of Kin*, Callahan recognizes the poet's work as locating Black experience and thereby constructing a broader, more nuanced understanding of American culture. The critic states: "Make no mistake about Harper's allegiance to a single complex diverse tradition. Much as he recognizes and heeds points of departure between American and Afro-American cultural patterns, Harper is a major American poet for the same reasons and in the same work he is a major Afro-American poet" ("Testifying Voice," 89).

Writing from Jimmy Carter's America, Callahan effectively renders a sketch of Harper's literary "two-ness," recognizing the poet's ability to integrate multiple musical, literary, and political pathways into his verse. He suggests that "Harper's purpose, like Du Bois at the turn of [the twentieth] century is to turn the notion (and fact) of double consciousness of racial and cultural polarity, into a strength and energy, a source of wholeness" (89). Embracing the complexity of Harper's poetic project and his exploration of the kinship mode, Callahan brings attention to the "convergent history" that emerges as a connective thread within *Images of Kin* and, by extension, throughout Harper's body of work.

Considered from this standpoint, overlooked and underexamined events from the American past represent an essential component of Harper's poetic project. As the poet develops and presents this particular historical mode throughout his verse, he collects the experiences of individuals, families, and groups that converge to form a nation. In Harper's poetry, history is understood to be more than an assemblage of events, chronologic presentation of facts, or arrangement of competing narratives designed to address the question, "how did we get here?" Instead, the poet works with an idea of "history" that serves as a conduit connecting conditions and experiences understood as "the present" to those recognized as "the past." Within Harper's body of work, history effectively functions as a "mode" that assumes and maintains a particular form, defining specific sites and spaces. Responding to events of the past in this way, Harper's poetry enacts and records a tangible, discernable history.

To undertake this project, the poet accesses and processes raw materials that comprise this historical mode as they emerge from his ongoing engagement with the "kinship mode." As such, Harper's poetic encounters with the past—what I'll call "generative history"—unfold through the contact he makes with "ancestors" while exploring sites within the American cultural space that he refers to as "the territory." Pursuing the past while moving along these pathways, Harper generates a varied set of historical content within his body of poetic work. For example, in the poem "Grandfather" Harper delivers a "family history" underscoring foundational elements of Black experience in the United States, while in "Here Where Coltrane Is" he works to connect circumstances and conditions across spatial and temporal planes, effectively "making history." In his autobiographical artist statement "My Poetic Technique and the Humanization of the American Audience," Harper acknowledges the critical attention his poetry has gained through its engagements with both the archival past and oral tradition: "I have gotten letters from 'friends' praising my knowledge of history" (30).

The poet's comment serves as a point of entry in his interview with literary critic David Lloyd as they discuss his poetry and its engagement with the past. At the outset of their wide-ranging discussion, Lloyd asks Harper to comment about "the role that history plays in [his] poetry." The poet responds: "I think the important thing about Americans is that they're not very good historians. . . . They're a very topical people and this is not to say some of them are not sincere. But on the issue of black [*sic*] Americans, in particular, the continuity of moral ideas gets thrown to the wind almost every turn . . . my vantage point on American matters is a bit askew, because [of] the dualism I bring . . . [to] a reading of mainstream America, as opposed to a reading of what one inherits" ("Interview with Michael S. Harper," 119).

Bringing attention to his work's engagement with the type of Du Boisian two-ness that Callahan considers in "Testifying Voices," Harper speaks to his poetry's treatment of history as a series of "open questions." Addressing matters of culture, custom, identity, and origin with Lloyd, the poet suggests that within his body of work, history does not serve as an official record for events drawn from *the past,* but instead becomes a means for exploring the convergence of the various *pasts* he sees forming and informing the modal dimensions of individual and collective memory. As their conversation continues, the poet informs Lloyd that his poetry's treatment of the past creates complexity ("or difficulty") within his verse. Through their exchange, Harper extends an account of the way that "generative history" informs his poetic project; at the same time, he scrutinizes progressive or consensus historiography and its adherence to a "historical record" constructed from archival documents. Harper interrogates the white supremacist foundations of what he describes as "mainstream" American history, calling to question prevailing presumptions that its sources are "inclusive" and "comprehensive."

Harper's poetic engagements with the past reflect and expand upon his exploration of the kinship mode. These connections become evident as Lloyd invites the poet to discuss his poem "Grandfather." Observing the poem's movement between "public and private perspectives," the critic suggests that like his work from the "Ruth's Blues" sequence, the poem "uses a piece of family history to explore the culture on a metaphorical level" (Lloyd, "Interview with Michael S. Harper," 126). Considering intersections between history and metaphor in this way, Harper and Lloyd's dialogue gestures toward the six-line aphorism found in several of the poet's collections:

> When there is no history
> there is no metaphor;
> a blind nation in storm

> mauls its own harbors:
> spermwhale, Indian, Black
> belted in these ruins. (2)

Part admonition, part incantation, these lines initially appear in Harper's work as as the opening and closing works of his third volume of verse, *Song: I Want a Witness*, under the titles of "Foreword: Song: *I Want a Witness*" and "Song: *I Want s Witness*." As such, they calculate a set of possibilities emerging from a space where history and metaphor converge. Registering at once a powerful presence and devastating absence, these lines effectively survey the destruction wrought in an environment where neither history nor metaphor are left unprocessed.

Throughout the course of his career, different versions and selected portions of "Song" appear in collections of Harper's verse. Within their various configurations, these lines comment on the brutality of American manifest destiny, extending the poet's call for reconsidering convenient, familiar ways that events of the past are understood and discussed as "history." Harper's speaker in "Song" enters, surveys, and records this expansive space, proclaiming "a blind nation in storm / mauls its own harbors." The poet does so, summoning American images of destruction, capture, and death—"spermwhale, Indian, Black"—effectively acknowledging an innate violence invested in the US national project.

With this three-part image delivering a snapshot of the transatlantic slave trade, whaling industry, and genocidal process presented as "the taming of the American West," the poet delivers a sketch of American empire construction. Identifying a systematic process at work, he positions its biproducts "belted in these ruins." Attending to the unknown and unseen possibilities embedded within these homegrown American historical horrors, Harper's speaker performs an act of restoration through literary recovery. Considering the weight and measure of the "spermwhale, Indian, Black" trinity in this way, the poet interrogates its capacity as "metaphor."

Considering the powerful relationship between "history" and "metaphor," the poet traces pathways of tragedy and waste within American experience using the underexamined yet overly determined figures of "spermwhale, Indian, Black." Serving as principal metaphors for environmental degradation, genocide, and slavery, the image ultimately speaks to William Carlos Williams's observations from *In the American Grain* that for Americans, "history begins for us with murder and enslavement, not with discovery" (39). In this way, each version of "Song" that the poet includes in his body of work bears witness to the devastation wrought by "a blind nation in storm." This message becomes amplified in the pattern of return and repetition that Harper's speaker establishes, shuttling between poetics and historiography, exploring connections between "convergent history" and "generative kinship." As such, the poet's song lines work to mark points of intersection that locate Black America within American experience writ large.

Through its various iterations, "Song" delivers a critique of what the poet calls "mainstream history." Addressing the imprint that white supremacist mythologies maintain within American history, Harper seeks to break the malignant stranglehold that their applied metaphor exerts on interpretations of national identity and the past. The poet presents history and metaphor as elements that operate in "antagonistic cooperation." Ralph Ellison explains his use of the term, likening it to the dynamic, improvisational interplay between jazz musicians. Presenting this vision of antagonistic cooperation in his essay "Going to the Territory," the novelist understands it as an essential component of American culture, developing his sense of the concept by drawing from literary critic Kenneth Burke's body of work. Ellison suggests that antagonistic cooperation simultaneously generates and reveals "hidden possibilities" embedded in American life. He goes on to state that its jazzlike impulses function "in such a way that not only is the original theme enhanced, but the listener is compelled to experience a feeling of catharsis" (129).

Ellison delivers a free-ranging discussion of US identity, culture, and history in "Going to the Territory," locating the influences of antagonistic cooperation within the founding documents of the United States, the results of the American Civil War, and the development of rock and roll. By doing so, the novelist effectively speaks to Harper's efforts to use his verse to recalibrate and reconceptualize American identity. Both writers account for ways in which antagonistic cooperation functions as a strategic response to hostile conditions and toxic environments experienced by people of African descent living within the United States, collectively and individually. Both Ellison and Harper maintain that without adequate metaphorical referents, "history"—which both writers regard as intersecting sites where imprints of the past make impressions on the present—can neither be contextualized nor understood.

By pursuing this modal approach to questions of history, Ellison and Harper ultimately bring attention to the ways in which Black expression—including literature, music, and vernacular practices—establishes connections with the force that the novelist refers to as "unwritten history." Clarifying his sense of this term in "Going to the Territory," Ellison writes that "we possess two basic versions of American history: one which is written and as neatly stylized as ancient myth, and the other unwritten and as chaotic and full of contradictions, changes of pace and surprises" (124). Comparing these two approaches to events and conditions of the past, Ellison states: "our unwritten history looms as [recorded history's] obscure alter ego" (126). Establishing this historical "two-ness" as a condition shaping Black experience in the United States as well as a broader sense of American culture, the novelist explains that "our unwritten history is always at work in the background to provide us with clues as to how this process of self-definition has worked in the past" (144).

Ellison's sense of unwritten history works to connect the disparate and, at times, divergent streams that he understands as American experience, speaking to the modal approach Harper's poetry brings to notions of "kinship" and "history." This connection is underscored when the novelist writes: "although repressed from our general knowledge of ourselves, [unwritten history] is always active in the shaping of events. It is always with us, questioning even when not accusing its acclaimed double . . . locked in mute argument which is likely to shock us when it becomes visible during periods of national stress" (124). Harper echoes this sentiment in his interview with David Lloyd. Addressing ties between his project and Ellison's, he plainly states: "it shouldn't be lost on me . . . that maybe I would have the responsibility for trying to do in the poetic area what Ellison did in fiction" ("Interview with Michael S. Harper," 123). Harper speaks to Ellison's modal sense of American history, extending the novelist's contention that "Americans can be notoriously selective in the exercise of historical memory" (Ellison, "Going to the Territory," 124). Considering the process of discovery and identity creation that takes place as individuals and groups develop "historical memory," Harper suggests that reconciling incongruities of the past requires "a solitary coming to terms with one's Americanness . . . [posing] an American problem for everybody" (Lloyd, "Interview with Michael S. Harper," 121).

Examining this "problem for everybody" throughout his poetic project, Harper ultimately addresses "the tragedy and waste" that he recognizes as components that inform both American history and Black experience in the United States. Tracing the color line in this way, the poet locates its imprint on political and cultural features comprising the American landscape. Mapping territories and contextualizing matters relating to Black life and Black expression in his poetry, Harper effectively identifies "acts of convergence" that bridge gaps separating what he calls "mainstream" history from Ellison's "unwritten history." In his essay "Poet as Kinsman," Robert Stepto discusses Harper's verse in similar terms. Stepto's essay presents the poet as a "master articulator" whose verse connects Black artists to Black experience through time. The critic understands Harper's work as reframing familiar subject matter—including concepts such as nation, family, and identity—within conversations about aesthetics, culture, and history. He recognizes the poet's engagement with "kin" as developing "metaphor" that simultaneously alters and realigns received notions about the American experience.

Understanding Harper's verse as simultaneously speaking to both the past and present, Stepto sees the poet's work with kinship as locating elements of a discernably Black past to generalized and extensively "whitened" notions of "American history." Undertaking this poetic exploration of how "history is made," Harper gathers disparate elements, integrating them into a distinct expressive mode. Pursuing "questions of history" in this way, the poet conducts a literary intervention where his verse examines material and subject matter that his "songlines" recognize as being "belted in these ruins." The poet gestures to the prospect of renewal that he sees emerging from a historiographic revision of this type. Reimagining Black life and "American experience" as it does, Harper's verse works to contextualize the convergent history the poet sees emerging from the elements that enter and inform his poetry. Acknowledging these complexities throughout his project, the poet delivers a conscientious exploration of the past that is personal and national or Black and American. These impulses, along with Harper's ability to incorporate them into his poetry, become particularly evident through a nine-line poem entitled "American History."

Initially published in *Dear John, Dear Coltrane,* "American History" speaks to the critique of "American mythic history" that Ralph Ellison delivers in his essay "Going to the Territory." This brief, powerful poem dedicated to noted Ellison scholar John F. Callahan engages the "radical juxtapositions" that the novelist associates with "the territory."[1] Connecting events to perspectives generated outside and away from the gaze of "mainstream history," Harper's poem pursues a vision of modal history:

> Those four black girls blown up
> in that Alabama church
> remind me of five hundred
> middle passage blacks,
> in a net, under water
> in Charleston harbor
> so *redcoats* wouldn't find them.
> Can't find what you can't see
> can you? (62)

In its first seven lines, "American History" delivers a gloss on the simultaneity of Black experience and American history. The poem establishes a set of connections that anticipate Ellison's notion of "unwritten history." With the poem implicitly contrasting Black experience in the United States with a national, "mainstream" American history, Harper's speaker enters a dialogue concerning matters of history, memory, and identity.

In this way, "American History" initiates a conversation about the scope of the American historical record and applied historiography by juxtaposing a well-documented and widely discussed act of anti-Black violence—the notorious Sunday, September 15, 1963, bombing of the 16th Street Baptist Church by white supremacists in Birmingham, Alabama—with an undocumented, undiscussed racially charged incident from the eighteenth century. The poet establishes a metaphorical threshold for engaging with the "tragedy" and "waste" that he understands as core elements of American experience. Harper's speaker provocatively describes the victims of the attack on Birmingham's 16th Street Baptist Church as "those four black girls blown up / in that Alabama church" (62). Introducing these figures and his subject matter through this colloquial use of determiners—"*those* girls" and "*that* church"—the poet implies, and even expects, that his audience should be familiar with what and whom he's referencing. His language—knowing and telling, as it does—suggests that despite the horrific brutality of the church bombing, its intended results—the killing and destruction of Black people—are, ultimately, commonplace events within American social and cultural history.

Underscoring this assertion and extending his meditation on American history and the US nation-building process, the poet matter-of-factly proclaims that the slain children "remind me" of "five hundred / middle passage blacks" drowned "in a net, under water / in Charleston harbor." Striking a cool, distanced pose while confronting genocidal violence, Harper's speaker casually gestures to another example of racialized mass murder in the United States. In "American History," the poet displays a hard-edged stoicism that informs without hysteria or hyperbole. Engaging the modal approach he brings to his literary project, Harper's speaker effectively presents his audience with a set of known facts. He identifies the legacies of slavery in acts of anti-Black hatred and violence as foundational elements in American national experience, or what the poem's title refers to as "American History." It is a devastating and abrupt comparison between two distinct sets of Black people, who, despite being removed from one another across space and time, become connected through the brutality of American racialized violence.

Within Harper's "American History," acts of racialized violence converge along intersections of memory and experience. They occur and "remind" the poet of the hazards faced by people of African descent in those parts of North America that have become the United States, from its earliest days into recent memory. Harper's speaker works to amend the nation's historical record, addressing a condition that Ellison describes as "historical amnesia." Using analytic categories such as geography, gender, and religion, the poet connects the deaths of "the four black girls" to those "five hundred middle passage blacks." The comparison addresses the reality of a selectively exercised, yet seemingly self-evident truth of American experience: Blackness renders death. In "American History," Harper's "blown up" girls, like his drowned Middle Passage Africans, ultimately illustrate the persistent desire of white America to terminate Black lives. These deaths stand for the "tragedy" and "waste" that the poet refers to while discussing American history in his interview with David Lloyd.

In the seventh line of "American History," however, Harper expands the poem's scope beyond a two-dimensional exploration of blackness and death. Engaging the convergent, modal history that informs his body of work, the poet presents the twisted logic informing the decision to drown enslaved Africans in Charleston Harbor "so *redcoats* wouldn't find them." The emphasis signifies a bitter irony he sees within the reasoning that would prompt Anglo-American colonial slave merchants to defy British imperial power by committing mass murder rather than having their "cargo" seized by the British Navy. The image of American merchants acting as calculating realists, choosing to deliver death rather than surrender "goods and profits," effectively recasts conventional representations of the American War for Independence and the Founding Fathers of the United States. Idealized notions of a nation forged by Freedom Fighters and the Enlightenment are eclipsed in "American History" as Harper's speaker tacitly acknowledges that "hiding" these "middle passage blacks" in this way eliminates the possibility that their bodies and labor would be used against the Americans' efforts to establish an independent nation if seized by "*redcoats.*"

In this way, the poem enters a broader exploration of the "historical record." Connecting the four black girls murdered in the Birmingham church bombing to Africans lost in the Middle Passage, Harper expands the interpretive range of the poem. Recognizing individual and collective aspects of these lives and deaths, the poet pursues questions about historiography and theories of history. These investigations resolve in the eighth and ninth lines of the poem: "Can't find what you can't see / can you?" Unfolding his inquiry in this way, Harper's speaker connects sight, location, and event, identifying the primacy of "can/can't" | "did/didn't" binaries within the nation-building project known as "American history."

Posing this recursive riddle at the end of the poem, the poet delivers an inwardly directed response to the explorations of Black death emerging from the first seven lines of "American History." Allowing terror and death in Alabama to resonate with terror and death in Charleston Harbor, Harper's poem delivers its literary critique of American mythic history. The poet "reminds" readers that violent acts perpetuated against people of African descent by white supremacists in the twentieth century resemble violent acts perpetuated against people of African descent by white supremacists in the eighteenth century. He suggests that Americans must learn and understand from this "history"; if they don't, they won't escape the destructive patterns of anti-Black violence.

"American History" challenges notions of American identity that manifest in "sight," "location," and "belief," found, for example, in variations on the "seeing is believing" adage, perhaps fully realized in Missouri's sobriquet as "The Show Me State." Throughout his poem, Harper delivers a subtle riff on the open-ended prompts that Francis Scott Key includes within the opening stanza of his poem "The Defense of Fort M'Henry":

> O! say can you *see,* by the dawn's early light,
> What so proudly we hail'd at the twilight's last gleaming,
> Whose broad stripes and bright stars through the perilous fight,
> O'er the ramparts we *watch'd,* were so gallantly streaming?
>   (Key 1814; emphasis added)[2]

These lines, easily recognized as lyrics from "The Star-Spangled Banner"—the US national anthem—also engage matters of sight and perception. Key's poetic concern for the whereabouts of the American flag at Fort McHenry during a British naval attack on Baltimore in the War of 1812 resembles the inquiries Harper's speaker makes about the Middle Passage Africans and Birmingham's four little girls in "American History." In both poems, the speakers raise questions that are, at once, rhetorical and informational as they go about expressing their intimate investment in American experience.

Considered from this perspective, "American History" delivers a multidimensional literary commentary on specific aspects of Black experience as well as conditions and contexts represented as the American past. As such, the poem questions the structure and orientation of standard American historical narratives, disrupting the ethos Ellison understands as informing "American mythic history." Recasting both the "Spirit of Seventy-Six" and the glory of 1812, Harper's poem effectively serves as an entry point to what the novelist calls the "underground of American unwritten history." The poet joins Ellison in working to offset an American tendency to "push significant details of our experience" out of view. Digging into the American underground, Harper's poem locates pieces of the nation's past, overlooked and disregarded by mainstream history. The excavation project that the poet undertakes in "American History" occurs, literally and figuratively, through his work's engagement with space and place.

The impact that geography makes within the poem becomes evident through its exploration of the concealed spaces where Harper's speaker locates the four Birmingham girls and the Middle Passage Africans. Whether submerged in Charleston Harbor or covered beneath the rubble of the 16th Street Baptist Church, these figures ultimately direct attention away from the "clean well-lit" sites allowed to stand for "mainstream American history" that include Bunker Hill, Fort McHenry, Mount Rushmore, the Rose Bowl, and others Harper's poem speaks to Ellison's assertion that "Americans live in a constant state of debate and contention . . . no matter what kinds of narrative, oral or written, are made in the reconstruction of our common experience" (124).

Recalling that "American History" was published in *Dear John, Dear Coltrane* some nine years before Ellison's exploration of unwritten history appeared in "Going to the Territory," the poem illustrates Harper's consistent use and application of modal history within his body of work. Read through Ellison's notion of underground history, the poem—like other work from Harper's debut volume, such as "The Guerrilla-Cong," "Ode to Tenochtitlan," "On Civil Disorders," and "A Mother Speaks: The Algiers Motel Incident, Detroit"—addresses questions relating to American identity and national experience. These poems map fissures and dividing lines within the United States as the Civil Rights phase of the Black Freedom Struggle closed and the Vietnam conflict continued. Delivering this poetic "State of the Union Address," Harper gained attention from a range of audiences as his verse found its way to the coffee tables and waiting rooms of Nixon's America through *Time* magazine's "Black America 1970" special issue. Featuring Jesse Jackson on its cover and Ellison's essay "What Would America Be Like Without Blacks," the April 6, 1970, issue of the news magazine—published two years after the assassination of Dr. Martin Luther King Jr.—included a piece entitled "Undaunted Pursuit of Fury" in its book review section.

Examining what Stephen E. Henderson would later refer to as "the New Black Poetry," the article considers works by a list of Black Arts Movement poets, including Amiri Baraka, Mari Evans, Nikki Giovanni, David Henderson, and Gwendolyn Brooks. As part of their survey of Black America, the editors at *Time* introduced many Americans to these Black poets and described Harper's verse as "elusive . . . [with] rhythms drawn from city sounds, African drumbeats, church responses, and the jazz of Coleman, Coltrane and Charlie ("Bird") Parker" (18). With this enthusiastic reading of *Dear John, Dear Coltrane,* "Undaunted Pursuit of Fury" recognized the poet's capacity to speak to and for various audiences, across the American color line. Witnessing "unwritten history" and working through "historical amnesia," Harper's poems offered a fresh perspective on conditions and circumstances that had become nearly ubiquitous in the United States during the era of televised network news-casts.

Delivering a poetic response invested in both Black America and the United States writ large, Harper's verse was hailed for its capacity to chronicle and comment on the escalation of US military operations in Vietnam, Laos, and Cambodia as well as the violent pursuit of individuals and groups involved in Black liberation movements by the FBI's counterintelligence program. Having poems from *Dear John, Dear Coltrane* reviewed in a publication like *Time* and enter into conversation with works by some of the day's most prominent Black poets ultimately provided Harper access to and greater visibility within wider American literary circles.

The story of *Dear John, Dear Coltrane*'s movement into print is well-documented and deeply embedded in Harper's professional aura. While the poet's rise was swift and his career long, the path he traveled immediately after leaving the University of Iowa offered little to indicate that his success was certain in the literary world. After returning to southern California from Iowa City in 1963, Harper taught English courses at California State, Los Angeles and Pasadena City College before moving to San Francisco and accepting a position at Contra Costa College. While teaching at this East Bay community college, Harper enjoyed the Bay Area jazz scene of the mid-1960s and met Shirley Buffington, whom he would marry in December 1965. During their time in San Francisco, the couple experienced three pregnancies that Shirley would bring to term. Their first son, Rolland, born in 1966, survived into adulthood, but their second and third children—Ruben Maasai Harper and Michael Steven Harper Jr.—suffered from acute respiratory issues and passed within hours of their births.

Harper and his family left the Bay Area in 1969, after the poet secured a pair of academic appointments in Portland, Oregon. While serving as poet-in-residence at Lewis and Clark College and holding a visiting lectureship in literature at Reed College, Harper came into contact with poet Phillip Levine. At Levine's urging he submitted the manuscript that would become *Dear John, Dear Coltrane* to the United States Poetry Prize competition. After much debate among the competition's judges, which included Gwendolyn Brooks, Harper was not named as winner of the contest.[3] However, fully convinced of his work's merit, Brooks rescued Harper's manuscript from the competition's slush pile and sent an encouraging letter to the poet, in which she told him, "you were my clear winner."

Following Brooks's recommendation, Harper submitted his manuscript to the University of Pittsburgh Press. Arriving with the working title "Black Spring," Harper's manuscript was published by that press as *Dear John, Dear*

Coltrane in early 1970. The volume received acclaim and was subsequently nominated for a National Book Award. In the same year, the poet accepted a position in the English Department at Brown University, which he held until his retirement in 2015. During his tenure at Brown, Harper participated in the American literary scene as a poet, teacher, and program administrator for the better part of five decades. In a biographical feature entitled "The Hardheaded Romantic," Anthony Walton explains that as Harper's voice became increasingly invested in both Black and American letters, the poet maintained a broad audience appeal that was rooted in "a hard-headed sense of the political realities of his day" (45).

Connecting Harper's poetry to the work of William Butler Yeats, Walton suggests that Harper's verse investigates the ways in which "[political] realities shape and, often, deform us" (45). As such, the poet's work launches an expansive investigation of Yeats's pronouncement that poetry is an outgrowth "of the quarrel with ourselves." Harper's poetry identifies collective and individual struggles with a set of all American "self-evident truths" that includes race, nation, and history. In this way, the poet and his project effectively work to recover and preserve artifacts and information endangered by these quarrels. Delivering accounts of personal and group experiences, Harper works to construct a more inclusive national past throughout his project, from *Dear John, Dear Coltrane* to *Use Trouble*.

Harper's poetic commitment to examining interpretive possibilities as they relate to the American past is evident in his early-career interview with John O'Brien. Explaining that within his work "myth is . . . open-ended," the poet expresses his own variation on Ellison's idea of unwritten history. Speaking against a backdrop of current events that includes the Watergate burglary and its cover-up, Angela Davis's legal battles in California, and Assata Shakur's arrest in New Jersey, Harper asserts that "*when* [myths] *are true, they* suggest new arrangements of human essentials based on contingent human experience, not on historical, systematic experience" (O'Brien, *Interviews with Black Writers*, 98, emphasis in original). Addressing enduring "questions of history" that he identifies as shaping and informing his poetic project, Harper extends his discussion of myth, history, and the American past. He presents O'Brien with a series of "resolutions" that he sees guiding his work and its exploration of a convergent, modal history.

Harper does so by stating that "if one has a vision of history as myth as lie, one has a closed reductive view of things," before continuing to say: "Of course the fantasy of white supremacist America . . . has always been a fantasy of a white country. Out of that kind of fantasy came genocide, Indian massacres, fugitive slave laws, manifest destiny, open door policies, Vietnam, Detroit, East

Saint Louis, Watts, the Mexican War, Chicago and the Democratic Convention of 1968" (98). Delivering this list of historically charged geographic sites, the poet performs a literary version of "taking names." At the same time, locating a series of intersecting points in this way, Harper maps the underground of American history. He marks and identifies the spatial, temporal boundaries defining his poetic engagement with "convergent history," effectively anticipating Ellison's assertion about the "twoness" American history: "one . . . neatly stylized as ancient myth, and the other . . . chaotic and full of contradiction" (Ellison, "Going to the Territory," 124).

Harper concludes this portion of his conversation with O'Brien with this assertion: "Myths are true when they suggest new arrangements of human essentials confirmed by past experience, when they invoke modes of connotation and implication, when they are open-ended" (98). The poet connects his efforts to access and integrate "open-ended" myth found in his verse through the pronouncement from the opening lines of "Song" that states: "Where there is no metaphor / there is no history." Simultaneously delivering a call to action and a poetic credo, these lines speak to Harper's extended dialogue with modal history and the interpretive possibilities that he pursues throughout his body of work. Read in this way, they provide a point of entry for interpreting the twenty-poem sequence found in the opening section of *History Is Your Own Heartbeat* that Harper entitles "Ruth's Blues."

Tracing points of convergence between "history" and "metaphor," this lengthy poetic cycle pursues a conversation about nation, identity, and the past. As such, "Ruth's Blues" becomes a vehicle for Harper to explore the imprint the color line makes on American life, through a set of poems examining personal and collective experiences, including those of the poet and members of his family. Delivering its in-depth exploration of both individual and national bodies, the "Ruth's Blues" sequence underscores connections between the poet, his verse, and "the underground of American history." The sequence surveys another level of "the territory," recording its physical and psychological features, while locating sites and spaces connecting family and nation.

This pattern becomes fully evident in "Blue Ruth: America," the opening poem in the "Ruth's Blues" sequence:

> I am telling you this:
> the tubes in your nose,
> in the esophagus,
> in the stomach;
> the small balloon
> attached to its end

> is your bleeding gullet;
> yellow in the canned
> sunshine of gauze,
> stitching, bedsores,
> Each tactoe cut
> sewn back
> is America:
> I am telling you this:
> *history is your own heartbeat.* (3)

Simultaneously surveying surfaces and interior portions of this female figure, these lines project the health and history of the American nation state onto Ruth's body. Held together by actual and metaphorical sutures, identifying "each tactoe cut / sewn back," Harper's speaker presents Ruth's vulnerable condition as a composite of the American experience. Opening with the unequivocal statement, "I am telling you this," the poet proclaims his intention to chart points of convergence between "history" and "metaphor," *in medias res.* With Harper's speaker "telling" about "this" as its starting point, "Blue Ruth: America" effectively maps a series of movements along the color line, locating intersections between body, nation, and family. Initiating the series of thick poetic descriptions and intersecting narratives that comprise the "Blue Ruth" cycle, the line becomes the foundation for Harper's intimate exploration of identity, experience, and embodiment.

In the sequence that follows, Harper delivers a detailed literary account of the complex family and medical situations that he and his wife, Shirley, confronted in the days leading to and following the birth of their fourth son, Patrice. On its surface, "Blue Ruth: America" recounts circumstances under which the poet's mother-in-law, Ruth McLaughlin Buffington, fell ill in Portland, Oregon during a March 1969 visit with her daughter, grandson, and son-in-law, prior to Patrice's birth. As the opening poem of the "Ruth's Blues" sequence unfolds, Harper's speaker addresses a fragile body through a web of medical equipment ("tubes," "balloons," "gauze") and family ties. His initial observations give way to a meditation on the well-being of the United States as he shuttles between two hospitals, one for the new mother and child and the other for Ruth and her "bleeding gullet." Exploring the pathways of family, embodiment, and belonging, this poem and those that follow in the "Blue Ruth: America" sequence identify wounds inflicted by the color line within and upon an American national body.

Considered from this perspective, Ruth's recovery from emergency gallbladder surgery underscores the poet's vision of an integrative, nation-building process in the mid-twentieth century United States, as does the healthy birth of his biracial child into a growing interracial family. Within the poem, Harper's speaker recognizes the "stitching, bedsores" and what is "sewn back" on Ruth's body as essential components in a project involving family, kinship, and nation. At the same time, the poet identifies "the canned / sunshine of gauze" covering his white, Midwestern mother-in-law as a shroud, eclipsing these deep divisions in her body. Ruth becomes "America," a nation he understands as being ravaged by the violence of its sustained military actions in Southeast Asia; racialized conflict in the streets of its cities; and the assassinations of Black liberation struggle figures, such as Medgar Evers, Malcolm X, Dr. Martin Luther King Jr., Fred Hampton, Mark Clark, and other members of the Black Panther Party.

In this way, the diminished capacity of this white woman's body and her bid for recovery offers encouragement to the Black poet. Observing her struggle with the weight of the color line, he acknowledges her commitment to the idea of family, expressed through her effort to visit her daughter and grandchildren. Harper's speaker in "Blue Ruth: America" imagines the advent of a new, powerful kinship mode, capable of interrupting entrenched patterns of American white supremacy. He witnesses Ruth resisting the systemic toxicities and dysfunctions that attack the nation like the maladies that besiege her organs. Proclaiming that her body "is America," Harper's speaker prepares to conclude the poem, reiterating his opening announcement, "I am telling you this" as preamble for the metaphor that resonates throughout the "Ruth's Blues" sequence and his whole body of work: *history is your own heartbeat.*

Building on this line, Robert Stepto suggests that "Blue Ruth: America" illustrates the poet's interest in exploring connections between "history" and "metaphor." He explains that "history is Ruth's own heartbeat in that the search for health and wholeness is bound to the rediscovery of a family, a self, and by extension, a culture or cultures unknown because of 'the un-wholeness'" (486). Understanding Harper's poetry as challenging projects invested in the pursuit of whiteness, the critic suggests: "Ruth's bandages are of necessity cultural or historical as well as familial . . . [They are] pieces of the same patchwork covering her 'national' wounds so that they may heal" (486). Writing in his "Poet as Kinsman" essay, Stepto extends this discussion of the "Ruth's Blues" sequence, by examining its fourteenth segment, "History as Bandages: Polka Dots and Moonbeams."

Presenting the poem as an example of Harper's sustained engagement with a convergent, modal history, "History as Bandages" ultimately stands as a foundational component of the poet's larger, longer literary project. According to Stepto, over the course of twenty-two lines the poem effectively annotates William Carlos William's statement from *In the American Grain* concerning "slavery and genocide." At the same time, the critic also sees it delivering a gloss on the "sperm whale, Indian, black" image that recurrently appears in various renditions of Harper's "Song." Stepto makes his case, focusing on imagery from the opening stanza of "History as Bandages":

> One is an igloo
> of whalebone and oil
> and a poisonous gas;
> one is a canoe under water
> laden with wild rice,
> grubs, and Indian arrows;
> one is a banjo
> packed with thin dirt
> in Richmond, Virginia:
> Gabriel: 1800;
> one is a round bubble
> of mustard rock
> broken on an Indian squaw;
> one is a print of a buffalo,
> bearded, masked, made
> musty skinned hair. (22)

For the critic, these lines confirm the historically rooted, literary mapping project that Harper pursues throughout his work. Tracing the imprint of genocide, slavery, and environmental degradation through the ebb and flow of American Manifest Destiny, the poem's opening stanza illustrates the poet's capacity to bundle images that convey his modal, generative vision of history.

Images from the opening stanza of "History as Bandages" contextualize, reiterate, and affirm Harper's vision. Entering the "underground of American history," the poet examines the "tragedy" and "loss" he sees within the nation's empire-building process. Summoning a poisoned igloo and sunken canoe "laden with wild rice," the poem's speaker offers an account of the degradation and carnage—both human and environmental—wrought by American colonization and conquest. Continuing along this pathway, he locates a banjo "packed with dirt," recalling the thwarted revolt planned for August 30, 1800, by enslaved people of African descent in Richmond, Virginia, organized by a man widely known as Gabriel Prosser.[4] Through the image Stepto describes as "the print of the buffalo," the poet accounts for the violence—including sexual violence—perpetrated against indigenous women in territories claimed by the United States.[5]

As the poem continues, images from the opening stanza raise questions that the poet begins addressing in the second stanza of "History as Bandages":

> The white rectangular
> patchwork covers all these
> national wounds kept
>
> secretly bound, at night,
> absorbing color and blood and bones
> of all shapes and disguises. (22)

With these six lines, Harper speaker opens a conversation about the process of "making history." He engages the distressing imagery from the poem's first stanza, identifying them as "national wounds." Referencing the gauze that envelops Ruth's body in "Blue Ruth: America," the poet describes a similar "white rectangular / patchwork" covering the various physical and psychological injuries suffered by the nation during its traumatic, bloody past. According to the poet, the "patchwork" of gauze that comes to stand for the "mainstream of American history" collects and conceals, "absorbing color and blood and bones."

Acting like a filter or screen, these "white" layers effectively eclipse the igloo, canoe, banjo, "mustard rock," and buffalo print imagery that arrives as the focus of Harper's poem. Applied to these "national wounds" in this way, the poet suggests that the projects of liberal, consensus history both consume and contain these maladies. Peeling back its dressings, which he describes as being "secretly bound, at night," the speaker understands its layers as preventing access to specific sites and experiences occurring within and upon the national body. "History as Bandages" raises questions about the response consensus historiography produces at the intersections of "history" and "metaphor" that the poet surveys in his various renderings of "Song."

"Blue Ruth: America," "History as Bandages," and other poems from the "Ruth's Blues" sequence perform a double duty within Harper's larger literary project. Connecting history and metaphor as they do, these poems also speak to questions relating to nation, experience, and identity. By doing so they become a vehicle for exploring "the underground of American unwritten history" and locating features within "the territory." As such, these works sustain Harper's efforts to counteract "whitewashings" of American history in his verse, effectively challenging the treatment that Black experience, Indigenous peoples, and other marginalized groups have traditionally received from and within the discourse of American history.

Harper discusses these poems and other work found in *History Is Your Own Heartbeat* in his interview with Abraham Chapman. Suggesting that the volume's title "means one must claim one's history," the poet explains that the collection also addresses the premise that "one must locate one's self in time and space and landscape so as to approximate what . . . one's tasks are, what one's responsibilities are to one's people, one's traditions, one's private and historical landscapes" (464). Constructing this list of "responsibilities," Harper gestures to the engagement his verse maintains with the poetry of William Butler Yeats. The imprint this dialogue makes on the poet's body of work becomes evident in several ways. For example, recalling that Yeats's collection *Responsibilities* carries the epigraph "In dreams begin responsibilities," Harper explores these notions, effectively reworking them, in "Nightmare Begins Responsibility."

Serving as the title of the poet's fifth volume of verse as well as an individual poem published in it, both the poem and the volume examine the individualized and collective history-making process. Where the poem explores the "painbreaking heartmadness" the poet and his wife experience having lost their two sons to "infant respiratory distress syndrome" within hours of their births, the eponymously title volume collects fragments of personal experience, connecting them to Black America and American life writ large.[6] The poet provides insight into his explorations of the terms "nightmare" and "responsibility" later in his interview with Chapman by suggesting that "what is needed is the creation of a new humanism, not the Americanism manifest in something called the American Dream, [which is] an American Nightmare! . . . The American Nightmare has to do with not being responsible to very complicated bloodlines that have gone into making of America. It begins with a conflict of worldviews and it begins with the recontextualization of what I call the essentialist vision" (494).

Harper works to address the "conflict of worldviews" and "essentialist vision" through his poetic project, producing a series of "history as" poems that dates from *History Is Your Own Heartbeat*. This considerable list of titles begins with "Sack 'a Woe: Gallstones as History," which appears in the "Ruth's Blues" sequence, along with "History as Bandages: Polka Dots and Moonbeams." These are just two of many similarly titled works from *History Is Your Own Heartbeat*. For example, the second section of the volume, which Harper calls "History as Personality," includes a poem entitled "The Morse Recount: History as Bridge, a Convention." The volume's third section, "High Modes," also features a series of "history as" poems, comprised by "History as Silence: Coroner's Song," "Aerial View: St. Louis, Missouri: History as Fly Paper," "Zeus Muse: History as Culture," and "History as Rat Poison: Gailgone: Gail's Song."

In their own way, each of these poems advances Harper's literary efforts to reconfigure historical conventions and widely accepted notions about events of the past. Transforming the idea of history as a staid, steady, and even predictable force, the poet instead understands it as a volatile component of experience, driven by and given to unexpected, if not entirely unpredictable, impulses. This project is further exemplified through the "history as" poems found in Harper's *Debridement* collection, such as "Rat Fever: History as Hallucination" and "History as Diabolical Materialism." These connections are amplified in the revised edition of *Debridement* that Harper produced with assistance from poet Ben Lerner.[7] They become evident as Harper speaks to the sustained engagement his verse maintains with the idea of history in his interview with Lerner from *To Cut Is to Heal,* the critical companion to the expanded version of *Debridement.*

Fielding questions about the structure of his volume and its explorations of myth, metaphor, and history in this interview, Harper discusses connections he sees between *Debridement*'s three poetic cycles. Identifying the collection's critique of systemic racism and white supremacist ideology, the poet contextualizes its discussions of John Brown's 1860 raid on the United States armory at Harpers Ferry, the life and career of novelist Richard Wright, and a Black Vietnam veteran's violent Detroit homecoming. The poet explains to Lerner that in both its original and revised versions, *Debridement* effectively presents "an alternative to the terrible choice [of either being killer or a victim] . . . and to be more discerning about the healing process" (24). As such, he understands these poems as promoting the "new humanism" he discusses with Chapman, effectively affirming his work's sustained commitment to developing a collective modal history.

Recalling that *Debridement* was initially conceived as a collection that combined poems published as *Song: I Want a Witness* with *Debridement*'s explorations of John Brown, Richard Wright, and Sargent John Henry Lewis ultimately provides occasion to consider Harper's most discussed "history as" poem, "History as Apple Tree." Arriving at the most intricately constructed simile of Harper's "history as" works, the poem serves as the foundational piece in Harper's "Photographs: Negatives" cycle. Over the course of this nine-poem sequence, the poet delivers an account of his young, growing family's adjustment to their new living arrangements on the East Coast. The cycle opens with a double epigraph, which allows the poet to set these poems within a literary variation on the call/ response patterns that support the blues and other modes of Black musical expression.

In the first epigraph of the "Photographs: Negatives" cycle, the poet issues his "call": "*Nightmare begins responsibility.*" After delivering this variation on Yeats's epigraph from *Responsibilities,* a "response" arrives in the improvisational riff on the meta-historical "sperm whale, Indian, black" image that Harper deploys in the first and final poems of the *Song: I Want a Witness* collection. Evoking the examination of history, memory, and metaphor that sustains this volume and his body of work, the poet writes,

> *The Indian is the root of an apple tree;*
> *history, symbol, presence: these voices*
> *are not lost on us, or them.* (43)

Building from the call/ response impulses he invests in these epigraphs, Harper's "Photographs: Negatives" cycle chronicles his family's efforts to make a home in the southeastern Massachusetts town of Dighton. Collecting images that he draws from their homesteading project, the poet brings attention to points of intersection where identity markers and institutional categories—including family, home, race, and region—imprint the New England landscape. In this way, the cemeteries, country lanes, woods, fields, and bogs that the poet encounters and observes with his wife and children through the course of the poetic sequence become entry points for the family's engagement with the region and its "unwritten history."

The "Photographs: Negatives" cycle explores presence and absence, change and continuity, using black-and-white photography as its vehicle. Exploring boundaries between "history" and "metaphor," poems in the sequence collect elements of the personal and collective past that the poet and members of his family locate in "New England." Measuring the depths of its displacements, they enter this environment, experiencing its "settlers," "colonists," and "ghosts," if not "pilgrims." With loss, discovery, and death always close at hand, the poet and his family are keenly aware of their status as new arrivals. Throughout this poetic series, Harper's high-contrast, enhanced-resolution imagery surveys and records the textures of New England culture and the region's layered traditions.

As a Black man with urban sensibilities rooted in Brooklyn and Los Angeles and a white woman from Minnesota, the poet and his wife observe Southeastern Massachusetts as people who are from "away." Having relocated to Dighton as an interracial couple from the West Coast with two biracial children born in California and Oregon, the Harpers presence effectively reframe dominant narratives and depictions of the region that would emphasize the imagined exclusivity of the region's Anglo-American historical past. Throughout the "Photographs: Negatives" cycle, the speaker accounts for his family's attempt to take root as transplants in unyielding, unfamiliar surroundings. Articulating their difference and distance from the region's standards, the poet and his family confront the historicized fantasies that inform New England culture as they process its complex, contemporary realities.

Understood in this way, poems from "Photographs: Negatives" examine the aggregate power invested in New England's prevailing cultural patterns. For example, three poems from the sequence consider distinct architectural features found in the New England colonial house that the poet and his family work to call their home. Through the course of "The Utility Room," "The Families Album," and "The Borning Room," Harper brings attention to irregularities in the configuration of the structure. In "The Families Album," the poet allows the house's "slanted pine floors," "crooked doorways," "covered well," and "dirt basement" to serve as reminders that he and his family are interlopers, who are *in* but not *of* this place. Similarly, Harper's commentary on their status as migrants to the region continues in "The Borning Room," when the speaker describes this space as one that, "the old tried to make it new / the new old" and then flatly asserts "we will not die here" (51). Similarly, the poet expresses the ambivalence that informs his relationship to New England and its idealized presumptions of whiteness in the "Photographs: Negatives" sequence's third poem of the "Night of Frost."

Seeking to improve their connections to the region's alien culture and landscape, the poet performs a set of rituals to claim space for himself and his family. In the opening stanza of "The Night of Frost," the poem's speaker narrates his trip to the mailbox of his new residence, declaring that "I walk out in the first / autumn frost" to "paste my decals /over the owner's name" (47). He goes on to celebrate his act of arrival by taking a nighttime tour of the surrounding countryside on foot. However, the poet becomes chagrined, sensing that his attempt to "re-label" and insert himself into this space neither improves his visibility nor advances his sense of attachment to southern New England.

In stanzas two and three, as he moves deeper into the landscape, the speaker encounters obstacles that prevent him from gaining a foothold upon and within this territory. Passing by its features, the "squat rock fence," "apple tree," "cyclops woman," and "tar paper roof" assume a sinister mien. As such, the poet's encounters with regional tropes effectively underscore his outsider position as both Black man and Black poet. He confirms his status in the fourth stanza of "Night of Frost":

> I walk as negative
> image over white crusted
> grave stones as my dark feet
> stamp their footprints. (47)

With these lines, the poet identifies himself as a Black man within a white-defined space. As a "negative/ image," he distinguishes himself from the New England countryside. With his Black body reduced to a pair of "dark feet" that "stamp" over "white crusted/ grave stones," the speaker articulates his presence within this charged landscape. Evoking black-and-white photography, New England becomes a contact sheet, tracing the pathways that the poet and his family have entered the "Old Colony."[8]

When read through their dialogues with the numerous photographic metaphors and imagery that appear in this sequence, the poet, his wife, and their sons are effectively "exposed"—like film—as their engagements with the New England landscape is "captured" through the "images" that comprise this poetic sequence. Poems from the "Photographs: Negatives" cycle chronicle the process by which the poet and his family "develop" relationships with and within the region and its history. Harper's verse collects and acknowledges the series of dramatic displacements—personal and collective—the poet sees encompassing New England. In poems such as "The Negatives," "Photographs," "Utility Room," and "Trays: A Portfolio," the poet explores and illustrates work that the poet and his spouse perform as they attempt to make their imprint upon this difficult, even hostile, environment.

Considered as acts of recovery, the nine poems in the "Photographs: Negatives" cycle chronicle and consider colonialism, white supremacy, and genocide as embedded legacies within the southeastern New England landscape. At the same time, the collection also documents recovery efforts that the poet and his spouse perform, responding to the deaths of their two infant sons. Throughout Harper's sequence, the couple explore their shared and individual grief with the assistance of various types of photographic equipment, including enlargers, chemical baths, fixes, hypos, agitators, and trays. By doing so, they seek to establish a homespace for themselves and their living sons, in addition to creating a resting place for their departed children.

Harper uses memory, photography, and poetics to enter the intimate spaces and record the difficult encounters that inform the generative history he constructs in the "Photographs: Negatives" cycle. Critic Robert Stepto considers the poet's sequence in his essay "After Modernism, After Hibernation: Michael Harper, Robert Hayden, and Jay Wright." Stepto suggests that throughout the poem the Harpers's late sons (Ruben and Michael) return to the couple on what the critic calls "the proof sheet of memory" (Harper and Stepto, *Chant of Saints*, 472). Registering themselves as "negatives" throughout the course of the cycle, the two departed children find their space within the family history.

The poet's engagement with the dead children becomes fully evident in "Trays: A Portfolio," the five-part poem that occupies the center point of the "Photographs: Negatives" cycle. In this portion of the sequence, the Harpers's departed sons hover just beyond their parents' field of vision. Their presence is especially strong as the couple works in their dark room, developing images of what Harper's speaker calls "our perfect family." As the poet and his spouse process film and print photographs, Ruben and Michael appear as

> *Two African veils*
> *on two sons*
> *clothed in their isolettes*
> *burn in a hospital.* (54)

The spectral images of their "two sons" effectively orient the poet and his spouse to their new environment and the current configuration of their family. Their entrances and departures give the poet pause to reflect on their brief lives. For example, in the third canto of "Trays," he recalls them as "two sons stoppered / from isolette / to incinerator." Later in this portion of the poem, Harper's speaker describes seeing "a child" tenuously appended to his spouse, "under her apron / as film develops / in her black and white eyes" (55).

In this way, as the couple struggles to resolve the grief and devastation of their losses through their pursuit of artistic expression, they create space for their family's history to resolve in metaphor. For instance, "Trays" advances the poet's claims for the redemptive possibilities of generative history, at both the collective and individual level. Capturing the ebb and flow of black/white, absence/presence, photograph/negative binaries, the poem extends the study of contrasts that Harper delivers throughout the sequence. Using the darkroom as their staging area, the poet and his spouse work to secure their purchase on the difficult emotional and historical landscape that they occupy. This strategy becomes evident in the poem's fourth canto, where the poet describes their collaboration to create a family archive: "we fight the dirt on the negatives / touch up with spotting liquid." This effort to produce what he calls a "contact: print" ultimately allows the couple to "blacken our negatives with light" (56).

The success of these joint endeavors becomes evident as "Trays" concludes with a hopeful image of the couple's two surviving sons, Roland and Patrice, playing together outside of the Dighton homestead "in a clot of pines." Observing his boys "roll in their bog / in a pool of grass" (57), Harper's speaker suggests that their adaptation to this environment has begun, and they are flourishing within it. Yet as the poet considers his sons, frolicking "in *their* bog" (emphasis added), he seems to question his children's capacity to maintain their inhibitions. While the boys would appear to have established their own sense of belonging within New England's contested space, Harper's speaker expresses caution, given the region's record of problematic engagements with people of color.

His trepidations awaken in the poem's fifth canto, where he recognizes the boys' play and movements as being fraught, even perilous: "each step trundled / each laugh bedded with blood" (57). Despite these concerns, however, and situating his surviving sons within southeastern New England as he does, the poet allows the boys to claim this space and make it their own. As a result, their play demonstrates the possibility for reshaping the region's history and geography. Emphasizing the significance of small interactions, the poet confirms a principal element of the modal history informing the sequence and his project as a whole.

Harper continues his explorations of generative history in the ninth and final poem of the "Photographs: Negatives" cycle, "History as Apple Tree." Engaging seventeenth-century Baptist theologian Roger Williams, the poem offers a reflection on the Harper family's late-twentieth-century efforts to settle in southern New England. Through the course of its five stanzas, the poet brings their attempt to establish roots on the "weed eaten farm" (57) in Dighton into dialogue with Williams's legacies as founder of the colony of Rhode Island and Providence Plantations. Acknowledging southern New England's diverse, multiracial past, the poet employs a range of voices to deliver his thick description of the territory now known as the state of Rhode Island. In the forty-nine lines comprising "History as Apple Tree," Harper's speaker comments on the construction of generative, modal history. At the same time, the poem's geographic focus makes connections across temporal boundaries with verse found in the "Photographs: Negative" cycle.

Working toward these ends, "History as Apple Tree" merges space, place, and experience with southern New England's land and waterways. The poet initiates this process in the poem's opening stanza:

> Cocumscussoc is my village,
> the western arm of Narragansett
> Bay; Canonicus chief sachem;
> black men escape into his tribe. (58)

With these four lines, Harper's speaker channels the voice of a Narragansett man who identifies himself as being from Cocumscussoc, the village where Roger Williams bargained with the sachem Canonicus to establish the region's first British trading post. Expanding the scope of the examination into race and identity found in the first eight poems of his "Photographs: Negative" cycle, the poet contextualizes his exploration of family history through a discussion of the British North American colonial project. Harper presents an alternate perspective on events imprinting the region and the development of the American nation.

Recalling that at the time of the poem's publication, great swaths of the nation's past were being processed in anticipation of the US bicentennial celebration, "History as Apple Tree" effectively resists and resets "whitewashed" notions of American history. While the cadence used by Harper's speaker in the poem's opening stanza merits scrutiny, it nevertheless contributes to the larger project of the "Photographs: Negative" cycle by making people of color within the region more visible, including the poet, his sons, and the speaker from Cocumscussoc. As such, "History as Apple Tree" adjusts alignments in which the American historical record and cultural landscape obscure the complex relationships and experiences connecting people of African and European descent to Indigenous populations along the "western arm of Narragansett / Bay." For example, writing "black men escape into his tribe" (58), the poet effectively remediates racial mythologies invested in the story of Anglo-American colonization. Moving like the poet's "dark feet" over "white crusted/ grave stones in "The Night of Frost," Harper's poem effectively disrupts the production of what Ellison calls "American mythic history."

Having established this foundation in its opening stanza, "History as Apple Tree" takes an abrupt turn as stanza two opens with the poet asking, "*How does patent not breed heresy?*" Shifting away from the speaker from Cocumscussoc, the poet gestures toward the circumstances that brought Williams into the territory that became Rhode Island. Recalling that Williams founded the colony by obtaining a "patent" from the Earl of Warwick's "Committee on Foreign Plantations," the speaker's question underscores the theologian's break with Massachusetts Bay Colony leaders regarding his positions on religious tolerance and the separation of church and state. Understanding the poetic query as being delivered by Williams, it not only makes reference to Warrick's colonial patent, but carries a critique of the "patent," or proprietary theocracy, that governed seventeenth-century Massachusetts.

However, before hairsplitting matters of Church and Crown overtake the poem, the Narragansett speaker returns, responding to Williams's query, delivering a detailed biographical sketch of the theologian from what may be understood as an indigenous perspective. The man from Cocumscussoc offers an annotated history of Rhode Island, explaining that Williams "came to my chief" while being "hunted by mad Puritans." He offers directions to the location of Williams's trading post and sketching out the business relationships Rhode Island's founder maintained with Massachusetts Bay Colony leaders, Richard Smith and John Winthrop:

With Winthrop he bought
An island, *Prudence;*
Two others, *Hope* and *Patience*
He named, though small.
His trading post at the cove
Smith's at another, close by. (58)

Later in the poem's third stanza, the man from Cocumscussoc provides an account of lacrosse games hosted by the Narragansetts: "Wampanoags, Cowesets, / Nipmucks, Niantics / Came by canoe for the games" (58). Describing these gatherings of the region's indigenous people, the poet comments on the multiethnic, multicultural landscape of seventeenth-century southern New England.

This stanza lends support to Robert Stepto's contention that "History as Apple Tree" and other poems in the "Photograph: Negatives" cycle "simultaneously" survey "a literal landscape, rich in lore and history (a south-of-Boston terrain) . . . and a figurative landscape of racial memory" (Harper and Stepto, *Chant of Saints*, 472). Writing in "After Modernism, After Hibernation," Stepto suggests that the poet is "aware of the private as well as public dimension of this ritual ground," writing that the "landscape of the poem is a historical field" (474). The critic effectively identifies Harper's movement through these geo-historical spaces as his seventeenth-century Narragansett speaker yields to a contemporary voice in the fourth stanza of "History as Apple Tree."

This temporal shift becomes evident as the poem engages the twentieth-century cultural and political landscapes that Harper maps in the first seven poems of "Photographs: Negatives." The poet bridges the centuries by invoking the legend of the "Roger Williams Root" and returning to the apple tree imagery found in the double-epigraph at the outset of the cycle.[9]

In your apple orchard
legend conjures Williams' name;
he was an apple tree.
Buried on his own lot
off Benefit Street
a giant apple tree grew;
two hundred years later,
when the grave was opened,
dust and root grew
in his human skeleton:
bones became apple tree. (59)

Summarizing the fantastic circumstances relating to the formation and discovery of "the Williams' Root," Harper's speaker assembles and examines a set of thematic occasions informing his poem's sense of modal history. Addressing matters of loss, recovery, and renewal, these lines literally and figuratively gesture toward the co-constructive interaction the poet sees connecting history and metaphor. The Williams Root accesses and engages the "underground of unwritten American history" while illustrating the poet's claims for the relationship between history and metaphor that appear in the multiple versions of "Song." While the assertion that "there is no history without metaphor" may be debated, the existence of the Williams Root effectively confirms that "where there IS History there IS metaphor."

The poet's exploration of history and metaphor continues in the fifth stanza of "History as Apple Tree." Claiming space for himself and his family within and upon the New England landscape, Harper witnesses the convergence of individual and collective history:

> As a black man I steal away
> in the night to the apple tree,
> place my arm in the rich grave,
> black sachem on a family plot,
> take up a chunk of apple root,
> let it become my skeleton,
> become my own myth: (59)

Having elected to "steal away" as he opens the final stanza of "History as Appletree," the poet evokes the legacy of the Spirituals and people of African descent escaping slavery. Harper's speaker moves through the southern New England countryside "in the night," as he does in "Night of Frost." However, at the conclusion of this poem, he leaves more than decals on a mailbox and footprints on the landscape.

Continuing his attempt to secure his family's place within the region, the poet digs into the land, aware of its past. As he excavates layers of genocide and enslavement from this "rich grave," Harper's speaker "takes up a chunk of apple root." Conjuring Roger Williams and the Williams Root, acting as "black sachem," he invests himself and his family into the landscape. Performing these rituals as the principal witness and participant in this process, he effectively resists the whitewash of history without metaphor. Consecrating his "family plot" in this way, Harper's speaker makes himself and his family visible in a space that would have them marked as "negatives."

Entering the land and grappling with its past as he does, the poet embraces this transformation. Experiencing a convergence of time, space, and identity,

Harper's speaker joins Williams, Canonicus, his spouse, and his four sons—present and departed—along with the man from Cocumscussoc as he "becomes [his] own myth." In this way, both "History as Appletree" and the "Photograph: Negatives" cycle arrive at their conclusion:

> my arm the historical branch,
> my name the bruised fruit,
> black human photograph: apple tree. (59)

Grafting roots to its trunk and branches, the poet assembles this family tree from his name and his body. As such, it casts a stark shadow, in the image of a "black human photograph," that arrives as both "history" and "apple tree." Harper's poem bears fruit as the speaker explores possibilities that collect as memory, belonging, and myth over the course of the "Photographs: Negatives" cycle.

Recognizing the commitment that Harper's project makes to various modes of personal and collective histories allows his modal poetic explorations to become more than literary examinations of the past. Creating engagements at the intersection of history and metaphor, Harper's verse moves beyond the limits of abstraction and analogy. For example, in "Archives," the poet delivers a detailed critique of the history making process that informs much of his body of work. Drawing on his experiences conducting research at the National Baseball Hall of Fame Library, "Archives" formulates a set of questions concerning documents and evidence rather than the metaphors and similes found in Harper's "History as" poems.

Written as Major League Baseball awkwardly approached the fortieth anniversary of Jackie Robinson breaking baseball's color line in 1947, "Archives" constructs a chronicle of Black baseball and Black baseball players, both on and away from the field. At the same time, marking Black baseball's relationship to both the Major Leagues and mainstream American history, the poem expands upon Ellison's notion of "mythic history" as it investigates his "unwritten history" concept.

"Archives" contributes to Harper's critique of discussions concerning the American past while making connections to the verse he includes in the "Photographs: Negatives" cycle. Both poems serve as examples of Harper's literary effort to map the American color line and chart race rituals and race relations in the nation. At the same time, through their engagements with aspects of still photography and motion pictures, these poems work to enhance the representations of Black life and American experience writ large. In this way, "Archives" speaks to historiographic questions regarding evidence, perspective, and perception that Harper raises in the closing lines of his poem "American History": "Can't find what you don't see / can you?" (62).

To pursue this line of inquiry, Harper's speaker opens the poem, matter-of-factly asserting that "Photos and clippings fade." With this pithy assessment of the documentary record serving as his starting point in "Archives," the poet speculates that his research trip to Cooperstown will ultimately become a survey of American unwritten history. Unable to document "why Josh Gibson died at thirty-/ five," while failing to obtain either "a real signature of Rube Foster" or "flicks of [Bob] Gibson as a Globe-/ trotter (45)," the poet ultimately confirms his suspicions. He is not surprised by his unsuccessful search for these pieces of Black baseball history within "the friendly confines" of this white-washed archive.

At the same time, even though its records are lacking, Harper's speaker expresses enthusiasm about the materials that *are* available to him. For example, in the second stanza of "Archives, " the poet moves through a "historical field" that is comprised of both Negro Leaguers and Black Major Leaguers. Claiming space within baseball's forgotten territories, his search effectively constructs a pattern of discovery and resolution. This dynamic becomes evident as the speaker, despite being unable to obtain a photograph of St. Louis Cardinals pitcher Bob Gibson during his days with the Harlem Globetrotters basketball team, celebrates the good fortune of finding a shot of the legendary hurler "captured, / for real, with Curt Flood, / eating steaks on a grill, / in a parking lot in spring / training" (45). Continuing to move through the "archives" in this way, the poet also describes a photo that transforms Hall of Fame slugger Reggie Jackson into "a mask / astride a roadster, a paltry / lid on a rainday with Vida Blue" (45).

Like the Gibson/ Flood photograph, this image allows the poet to consider another pair of Black teammates. Both photos capture pitcher-outfielder duos that made vital contributions to dominant teams of their respective eras. Along with the shot of Gibson and Flood, the Jackson/Blue photograph provides Harper's speaker with evidence that relationships between Black baseball players reached beyond the clubhouse.[10] Collecting images and describing them as he does, the poet creates a kaleidoscopic display of modal history. These poetic components ultimately collide and reverberate within the discussions Harper constructs in the third and fourth stanzas of his poem.

Recalling that while "Archives" was published in *Honorable Amendments,* it initially appeared in *TriQuarterly* 65 along with Harper's interview with David Lloyd and four other poems: "Heat," "Presidential Quotes," "The Deer," and "Study Windows." In the course of his interview with the poet,

Lloyd describes Harper's poetry as being "connected to writers like Paul Laurence Dunbar, Robert Hayden, and Sterling Brown, who have not yet received
their due from mainstream American critics . . . [as well as other] black (sic)
American heroes like Jackie Robinson or Willie Mays." Lloyd goes on to ask
the poet: "Are you rewriting American history in some way?" ("Interview with
Michael S. Harper," 119). Offering insight to his project in "Archives" and other
poems that treat "questions of history," Harper responds: "I'm certainly giving
my version of the history. I mean I share that vision with a lot of other people.
But we're dealing with some people in the popular theater who are never seen
as material for real literary recovery. . . . There is a tendency in this country
toward topicality but not toward continuity. . . . I'd like to remind readers about
[these figures] not so much because their exploits were unseen but that the context wasn't understood" (120).

   This ethos informs "Archives" and its effort to recount how Hall of Famer
"Frank Robinson's loaded automatic / put him under arrest" while he was
a member of the Cincinnati Reds. It also imprints Harper's description of
Jackie Robinson "Stealing home / in public" carrying "the whole Civil War/
on his back and pigeon-toes" (46). In this way, the poet weighs materials and
artifacts he can (and can't) find in Cooperstown, bearing witness for Black lives
lived within Jim Crow America. Inspecting "clippings of the rest / of Negro
America," the speaker of the poem ultimately shifts his gaze away from the exploits of ballplayers, effectively bringing consideration to questions concerned
with the archive and its capacity to adequately present and represent Black
experience.

   In the fifth stanza of "Archives," Harper considers the way Black baseball
is discussed, on those occasions when it receives attention from the makers of
mainstream American history. Punctuating this attention's intersection with the
white supremacist mythology invested in American national myths, the poet
writes,

> On PBS the documentaries,
> one trailer sideshow,
> a whole hall of oral history
> in transcriptions
> of black and white. (46)

To counter these reductive impulses, Harper's speaker conjures images of "the
black World Series in Comiskey [Park]." Moving deeper into the "territory"
of Black America, he enters a "hall of oral history," addressing the complexity of Black life in segregated America. He does so, describing the home of

the Chicago White Sox as "Full of chicken, zoot suits, / trainfare from every-where / but endorsements, turnstyles" (46).

As "Archives" reaches its conclusion, the poet remains in the Windy City. In the poem's seventh and final stanza, he draws a quote from Chicago Cubs great Ernie Banks. Delivering the tagline synonymous with "Mr. Cub" and his enthusiastic devotion to the game, "Let's play two" (46), the poet allows Banks to have the final word. Aware that the Hall of Famer began his professional baseball career in the Negro Leagues with the Kansas City Monarchs before he became the first Black player on the Cubs, Harper calls upon oral tradition that so often eludes the historical record. At the same time, Banks's catch phrase also resonates with the "twoness" of Black life in the United States, as framed by Du Boisian double consciousness. In this way, Harper's poem creates space for Black people to locate and contextualize themselves and their experience within and against a hostile historical field.

CHAPTER 4

Pursuance (Black Music)

Throughout his eleven volumes of published verse, Michael S. Harper develops an extended dialogue with the sounds, voices, and figures that he locates within the Black music continuum. Tracing the imprint Black musicians and their artistic legacies have made on both Black expression and American experience, Harper's verse explores various modes of blues-rooted music. Over the course of his project, while executing a series of call-and-response patterns, the poet captures the melodies, rhythms, tones, and colors of Black music. Addressing the music's connections to both Black identity and American culture writ large, Harper's poems engage impulses that Black music scholar Dwight Andrews refers to as the "blues aesthetic" in his essay "From Black to Blues: Towards a Blues Aesthetic."[1] In other words, Harper's poetry participates in a modal conversation with both Black musical expression and Black musicians.

From the works that appeared in small journals during the mid-1960s to the poems he published in the second decade of the twenty-first century, Harper's verse examines cadences, harmonies, and improvisational components of the Black musical form widely known as "jazz." Working with both the music and its makers, the poet speaks to and draws from the Black music continuum. Harper's literary project explores possibilities for individual expression while acknowledging the necessity of collective representation. Beginning with the publication of his first volume of verse, *Dear John, Dear Coltrane*, much of the critical and scholarly attention given to Harper's poetry focuses on its engagements with Black music. Consistently recognizing the capacity of blues-rooted music to capture and convey Black experience, Harper's verse effectively locates and identifies features found within Black America while tracing the imprint that Black artists have made upon the broader American cultural landscape.

Collecting endorsements as he pursued this project, described through-out his career as a "jazz poet," Harper's work is consistently categorized as "jazz poetry." Both the poet and his verse were widely celebrated as such. Harper worked with these labels, welcoming the attention they brought him, ranging from the praise his poetry received in *Time* magazine's 1970 special volume on Black America ("Undaunted Pursuit of Fury") to Herman Beavers' "When There Is No Song, There is No History: The Ephemeral Poetics of Austerlitz and Harper's *Double Take*." delivered at the University of Missouri's 2013 Michael S. Harper Symposium. Harper's willingness to be read in these terms is confirmed, for example, in a mid-career interview with critic Reginald Martin. When Martin asked the poet if he saw connections between his work and the jazz tradition, Harper unequivocally states: "Yes, I do. I consider my-self a musical poet, and to a musical poet individuality is most important and I suppose that's jazz-like" (Martin, "Interview with Michael S. Harper," 442).

In his introduction to the 2014 special volume of the *Worcester Review* examining Michael Harper's poetry, Anthony Walton recognizes the com-plex set of relationships that history and kinship maintain with blues-rooted expression and Black music throughout the poet's body of work. Discussing "Dear John, Dear Coltrane," Walton considers the title piece of Harper's first published volume as more than a praise poem to a beloved musician. Instead, he presents the work as a poetic portrait, which Harper dedicates to an artistic kinsmen. Aware of the poet's relationship with Coltrane's music, Walton ex-plores the poem in terms of Harper's ongoing examination of Black music's connections to Black experience. Building upon Stephen E. Henderson's read-ing of "Dear John, Dear Coltrane" in *Understanding the New Black Poetry,* Walton sets the poet's literary representation of Coltrane and his musical ex-periments into conversation with social realities present within Black America, including landlessness and lynching: "Harper was moved to write ["Dear John, Dear Coltrane"] after reading of the 1899 lynching of Sam Hose near New-man, Georgia" (Walton, "Introduction: Sacred Geometry," 91). He identifies the poet's sense of Coltrane as a Black artist with roots in Black culture and the rural South, suggesting that Harper's poem presents the musician "as a 'witness to this love/ in this calm fallow / of these minds' . . . thus referring to a people without a land" (91).

Walton understands "Dear John, Dear Coltrane" as a nuanced portrait of the musician that recognizes Coltrane as more than a jazz icon. His interpreta-tion of the poem acknowledges Coltrane as a concerned, conscious Black artist. Walton's reading of the poem also sees Harper recognizing the musician and his work as the realization of the aesthetic ideal and transformational ethos that emerge from the poet's verse as "a love supreme." This three-word phrase, drawn from Coltrane's recorded masterpiece "A Love Supreme," appears as a chant, refrain, and mantra throughout Harper's body of work. Gesturing toward the apex of the expressive mode that the poet seeks to attain through his verse, "a love supreme" articulates aesthetic possibility while becoming a mode of delivering blessings and actualizing a way of being in the world.

In his interview with John O'Brien, Harper discusses the imprint Coltrane and his music have made on his literary project. When O'Brien asks about the "very special way" that the musician "influenced" his work, Harper replies: "I loved John Coltrane and I loved his music. I loved the kind of intensity he brought to his playing and I loved his commitment . . . potency is obviously a great part of Coltrane's playing and of the music of contemporary black [sic] musicians . . . I think the most important thing to remember is that jazz and blues are open-ended forms and not programmatic and not abstract. They're modal. And by modality, I mean some very complicated perceptual and moral things. . . . John Coltrane was a modal musician. [His music has] the kind of energy it takes to break oppressive conditions, oppressive musical structures, and oppressive societal situations" (97).

Recognizing Coltrane as both a Black artist and Black musician, Harper provides O'Brien with a sense of the impact that the saxophonist's modal explorations of the blues have on his own poetic project. The poet suggests that, like Coltrane, he seeks to recast familiar structures and conditions through his art. Understanding Harper's Coltrane figure and the "love supreme" ethos as connective threads in his body of work allows the poet to refine and articulate the range of musical visions and voicings emerging from his verse. This sensibility also is present in Harper's portraits of swing and bebop figures from the 1940s like Charlie Parker, Coleman Hawkins, Lester Young, and Billie Holiday. It extends into his poetic profiles of Hard Bop, Cool, and avant-garde jazz musicians from the 1950s and '60s, such as Miles Davis, Bud Powell, and Eric Dolphy, also found throughout his work.

Harper's jazz poems and poetic explorations of Black music access the fabric of Black America. Through his depictions of individual musicians and their work, the poet contextualizes the music and the musicians from the second phase of the "Jazz Age."[2] In Harper's verse, these Black artists stand as instructive figures, whose artwork respond to challenges faced by people of African descent, living in the United States during the Jim Crow era. Recognizing the capacity of their blues-rooted, Black expression to deliver a collectivized message through a singular voice, Harper's verse captures the responsive, improvised eloquence that is Black music's animating force. His jazz poems enter into an extended conversation concerning aesthetics, nation, and identity.

Harper writes about these connections in "Introducing the Blues," the summary introduction to a special supplement on Black poetry that he edited for *American Poetry Review*. Addressing the intimate relationship that Black music has with Black letters and within American life, the poet states: "In this short essay, a reading list is also a good record player. Black expression demands that people *do*—that people create themselves—that process is dynamic, that *both/and* is always better than *either/or*" (19, emphasis in original). Like his own verse, the poems in this "Folio of Black Poets"—which includes work by Alvin Aubert, Lucille Clifton, Everett Hoagland, and Sherley Anne Williams—speak to foundational elements of Black experience and expression, especially the blues. Harper's explorations of relationships connecting Black music and Black letters is not a passing interest. The blues roots of Harper's poetic project are found throughout his body of work, going back to the Master of Arts thesis he submitted under the title "Blues and Laughter" at the University of Iowa in 1963.

Although Harper has dismissed "Blues and Laughter" as apprentice work,[3] titles listed in the collection's table of contents clearly speak to his ambition to have his work enter a poetic conversation with jazz and other forms of blues-rooted music. To underscore this aspect of his project, the collection opens with an epigraph: "Can he play the blues?" In the seventeen poems in this volume, Harper is intent on having his readers answer in the affirmative. He evokes the blues idiom with poems such as "Blues Minor" and "Phoenix or All the Things You Are." Poems such as "To Billie Holiday" and "Bebop International" render portraits of jazz greats and explore his sense of aesthetic kinship with them. Throughout "Blues and Laughter," Harper investigates possibilities for rendering modal expression within his poetic project while exploring the kinship and experiential archive that he locates within Black music.

Harper's effort to connect with the Black music continuum in "Blues and Laughter" is best illustrated by the version of the poem "Alone" that he includes in this collection. Appearing as five three-line stanzas, "Alone" delivers a melancholy meditation on romantic rebuff. Seeking to confirm his credentials as a world-weary traveler, the poem's speaker delivers a collection of clichéd images, which include scotch, lost love, and the loneliness of Miles Davis's trumpet. As such, "Alone" might have been easily dismissed if Harper had not revised the work and included a spare, three-line version of the poem in his *Dear John, Dear Coltrane* collection, some seven years later. Comparing the two versions of "Alone," Harper's interest in moving beyond the expressive limits of a stereotypical, bohemian, "jazz poem" becomes evident. His revisions reflect his understanding of the blues tradition as a mode of expression, rather than an emotionally constructed sensibility.

In "My Poetic Technique," Harper identifies "Alone" as a product of his days in Iowa City and confirms his interest in honing its shape and form. Discussing his writing process and alluding to the drastic cuts he made to the poem's original version, he writes: "My first and only poem on the worksheet in the poetry class was a poem dedicated to Miles Davis, 'Alone,' which I've since cut down to three lines. It was my bible. How would it be to solo with the great tradition of the big bands honking you on? Could one do it in a poem? I'd taken my survey courses, studied my Donne and Shakespeare . . . and gone to American literature without Frederick Douglass, Du Bois, Johnson or Toomer . . . and searched for the cadence of street talk in the inner ear of the great musicians" (29).

Having retained just three of the fifteen lines from the "Blues and Laughter" version of "Alone," Harper recognizes the edited version of the poem as a counterpoint to popular, market-driven impulses that consistently ask for Black music to be played "bigger," "louder," and "stronger." He effectively allows "Alone" to speak back to the "white noise" of the American literary canon that has consistently muted the voices of Black writers, from Phillis Wheatley to Frederick Douglass to Jean Toomer and Gwendolyn Brooks. Pursuing this course of action, the poet seeks to break through this wall of sound, employing a strategy that he calls the "cadence of street talk in the inner ear of the great musicians." In this way, his editorial work on "Alone" ultimately responds to the question he raises at the outset of "Blues and Laughter," confirming that he is, indeed, able to "play the blues."

The version of "Alone" from *Dear John, Dear Coltrane* arrives, framed by the tidy dedication, "for Miles Davis." The poem allows Harper to demonstrate his commitment to exploring the possibilities of Black music and blues-rooted expression. It also stands as a testament to the intense scrutiny that the poet brings to his project:

> A friend told me
> He'd risen above jazz
> I leave him there (5)

With these lines, Harper establishes a set of essential connections that he sees informing the blues. Appearing on the page as a deceptively simple three-line poem, "Alone" effectively speaks back to the definition of the blues that Ralph Ellison famously delivers in "Richard Wright's Blues." Considering blues as both a musical form and an expressive mode, Ellison famously asserts: "The blues is an impulse to keep the painful details and episodes of a brutal experience alive in one's aching consciousness, to finger its jagged grain, and to transcend it, not by the consolation of philosophy but by squeezing from it a near-tragic, near-comic lyricism. As a form, the blues is an autobiographical chronicle of personal catastrophe expressed lyrically" (78–79).

Speaking to this type of intense, condensed experience, the poem's compressed language resonates with Ellison's definition and understanding of the blues. At the same time, "Alone" also prompts a series of questions: Who is this "friend?" Is the "friend" Miles Davis? What is it to have "risen above jazz?" Where is the space "above jazz?" Who does the poet wish to "leave?" Why leave him "there?" Both poem and poet ultimately "leave" readers "alone" to contemplate their responses to these questions. These questions bring attention to structural elements of "Alone," which underscore its multipoint engagement with the blues. On a very basic level, the poem's three-line composition recalls the standard, three-chord blues progression: I, V, IV.

Rising and falling on the page as it does, "Alone" also resembles the three valves of Miles Davis's trumpet. Like trumpet valves, these lines become animated and differentiated by various combinations of stress (embouchure) and timing (fingerings). The poet explores the modal possibilities invested in these relationships through the course of the nine distinct readings of "Alone" found on *Our Book on Trane: The Yaddo Sessions*, a recorded collaboration between the poet and reed player Paul Austerlitz. Exploring a set of varied cadences and inflections that they locate within "Alone," Harper and Austerlitz read and play a series of poetic possibilities, allowing them to generate nine distinct, recorded interpretations of the poem's three lines.

Through the course of their exchange, poet and musician engage in a series of call-and-response treatments of "Alone," rendering it as both a poem and a mode. With the two artists arranging and re-arranging their respective approaches to the poem, shifting rhythms and phrasings, they demonstrate the transcendent capacities of improvisation, repetition, and difference. Exploring the jazz impulses of "Alone," Harper's voice and Austerlitz's bass clarinet enter the poem, interpreting and reinterpreting its lines through the recording. Working in this way, they allow the poem itself to respond to their treatment, effectively answering the question Harper raises at the outset of "Blues and Laughter—"can he play the blues?"—in the affirmative.

Reading, playing, and repeating "Alone" as they do, poet and musician both deliver variations on the poem, conveying its lines with expressions of incredulity, resignation, and amused skepticism. Performing the poem in short, staccato bursts, Harper and Austerlitz punctuate their recitations of "Alone," using pronounced hesitations and emphatic remonstrations. In their ninth and final performance of the poem, Harper sings the final line, "I leave him there," investing it with a melody that approximates the "a love supreme" chant John Coltrane vocalizes in the closing bars of "Acknowledgment," the first movement of his composition "A Love Supreme."

By doing so, the poet demonstrates his commitment to exploring and articulating the possibilities he understands to be invested in "a love supreme." Treating this modal notion and spiritual concept as an aesthetic apex of blues-rooted expression, the poet works with his musical collaborator, effectively illustrating the poem's transcendent possibilities. By combining forces, the two artists realize the poem's expressive capacities. In this way, Harper and Austerlitz simultaneously interpret, revise, and embrace "Alone" and its modal engagements with the concepts of jazz and kinship.

Harper pursues an alternate approach to producing blues-rooted, modal verse in "For Bud," another "jazz poem" from *Dear John, Dear Coltrane*. Like "Alone," this well-known example of the poet's early work maintains a set of clear connections to the Black music continuum. While both poems deliver portraits of groundbreaking jazz musicians that incorporate literary representations of musical instruments into their structure, they do so in decidedly different ways. "Alone," written for Miles Davis, appears on the page in three lines that resemble the valves of a trumpet. "For Bud," dedicated to the memory of bebop-era pianist Bud Powell, also makes reference to its subject's instrument. Harper's speaker brings attention to the pianist's "strong left hand," which reputedly had a range of one and a half octaves. The poem is nineteen lines in length, equaling the total number of piano keys—major and minor—below middle C that the pianist's left hand was able to span.

Originally published in the February 1968 volume of *Poetry*, "For Bud" differs from "Alone" in the way that it elegizes Powell, who died in the summer of 1966 at the age of forty-one, after suffering the effects of tuberculosis, alcoholism, and malnutrition. Unlike the enigmatic, modal praise poem that Harper dedicates to Miles Davis, "For Bud" situates its subject within a discernable set of spatial, temporal, and experiential boundaries. The poem offers an account of the expectations that accompanied Powell, as his reputation grew—beginning at the age of ten—while playing rent parties and other social gatherings in Harlem. It recognizes the pianist as following in the footsteps of his father, an accomplished New York stride-style pianist, as well as those of his brother William, a notable trumpet player. "For Bud" also understands the celebrity Powell gained among Black musicians as a virtuoso prodigy while establishing himself on the Uptown jazz scene. Harper's poem does so, acknowledging the pianist as participating in late-night jam sessions during the early forties, at the outset of the bebop movement, while he received mentoring on his instrument by both Thelonious Monk and Art Tatum.

At the age of nineteen, Powell accepted an offer to play piano in an orchestra led by former Duke Ellington sideman Cootie Williams. The pianist held this seat until January 1945, when he was beaten and detained by police in Philadelphia. The beating affected Powell for the remainder of his life. Plagued by chronic headaches, mood swings, and periods of psychological distress, the pianist was institutionalized, ultimately receiving electroconvulsive therapy treatments at the Bellevue Hospital Center in Manhattan and the Creedmoor Psychiatric Center in Queens. Despite these struggles, Powell contributed to the bebop movement as a composer and bandleader, in addition to doing side work with numerous ensembles, in both studios and clubs. Notably, he was the inspiration for Thelonious Monk's composition "In Walked Bud," a tribute piece that Monk recorded several times during his career, beginning in 1947.

Powell performed and recorded with a list of highly accomplished contemporaries, including Art Blakey, Dexter Gordon, Sonny Rollins, and Charlie "Bird" Parker. Despite maintaining a famously contentious relationship with Parker, in the spring of 1953 Bird invited Powell to play piano with him and an all-star group featuring Dizzy Gillespie (trumpet), Charles Mingus (bass), and Max Roach (drums). These five pioneering Black musicians performed this single show engagement in Toronto as "The Quintet." Their concert—the only appearance these musicians would make as an ensemble—was recorded and ultimately distributed as the legendary *Jazz at Massey Hall* album. Powell also contributed to other acclaimed recording sessions of the era, and his playing was featured on cuts like "Bouncing with Bud," "Glass Enclosure," and "Un Poco Loco."

Harper engages elements of the "convergent history" shaping and informing Powell's life and musical career in "For Bud." Throughout this impressionistic elegy, the poet animates points of intersection linking the pianist's music to his personal experiences. In this meditative poetic sketch, Harper's Powell figure becomes a "mode," effectively illustrating the modal approach the poet uses in his jazz poetry. Harper provides a measure of context for this dynamic during an interview with Abraham Chapman where he explains that "a mode reveals its own truth on its own terms: a mode is true unto itself" ("An Interview with Michael S. Harper," 465).

At the same time, in "For Bud," Harper's speaker follows several pathways through the Black music continuum. The poem marks and measures the broad range of expressive possibilities that the poet locates within blues-rooted music. For example, "Alone," with its three stark, declarative statements, approximating the allusive musical style of Miles Davis, raises more questions than it resolves. "For Bud," on the other hand, constructs a mode from the inquiries that the poet develops through his observations of the pianist's life and music.

Evoking Powell's approach to the keyboard, questions form and pass through the course of "For Bud" without direct response. This modal shift from statements to questions is evident at the outset of the poem:

> Could it be, Bud
> that in slow galvanized
> fingers beauty seeped
> into *bop*, like Bird
> *weed* and Diz clowned—
> Sugar waltzing
> back into dynamite,
> sweetest left hook you
> ever dug baby. . . . (18)

Opening the poem with a note of curious inquiry, "Could it be, Bud," Harper's speaker conveys a sense of the possibility he finds within Powell's music. The poet moves on, identifying the pianist's sense of musical process, describing his technique as "slow galvanized / fingers beauty seeped into *bop*." The poem continues and Harper's speaker describes the work that Powell's left hand performed while at the keyboard.[4] Correlating the pianist's movements to those of boxing champion Sugar Ray Robinson, the poet connects the boxer's footwork ("Sugar waltzing") and punching power ("sweetest left hook you / ever dug, baby") to Powell's ability to create runs using his left hand.

"For Bud" continues, surveying the foundations of Powell's musical project and probing its engagement with expressive possibility. In the poem's next six lines, Harper's speaker surveys this sonic space:

> could it violate violence
> Bud, like Leadbelly's
> chaingang chuckle,
> the candied yam
> twelve string clutch
> of all blues (18)

Aware of the pianist's reputation for pugnacious engagement with authority figures—including police officers and orderlies at mental health facilities—the poet underscores connections between Powell's "strong left hand" and that of Sugar Ray Robinson. At the same time, gesturing to the twelve-string guitar styling of blues legend Huddie "Lead Belly" Ledbetter, Harper's speaker links Powell's playing to Lead Belly's legacy. Making what would appear to be an unlikely association between the applied techniques of a stride pianist and those of the guitarist, the poet expands the scope of their ties beyond a shared sense of blues fundamentals. "For Bud" not only identifies these two Black musicians' technical prowess, but also at the same time tacitly acknowledges their distinct contributions to the dynamic mid-twentieth-century New York music scene. The poem also recognizes the musicians' shared experiences as Black men living within the parameters of mid-twentieth century Jim Crow America, which—for both Powell and Ledbetter—included being institutionalized at New York's Bellevue Hospital.

"For Bud" concludes as Harper's speaker eulogizes Powell in the poem's final three lines. Building on the poem's allusions to "Bird," "Diz," and "Leadbelly" while referencing the explosive power of the pianist's music ("dynamite," "left hook," "violate violence," "chain gang chuckle"), the poet responds to the open-ended inquiries that he directs toward the pianist at the outset of the poem:

> there's no rain
> anywhere, soft
> enough for you. (18)

Having situated the pianist within the Black music continuum and identifying his contributions to the tradition, Harper's speaker addresses the transcendent beauty of Powell's artistry with these lines. The poet's modal imagery renders a responsive portrait of the pianist's life and his music. Accounting for the turbulence that followed Powell away from his piano bench and the bandstand, "For Bud" effectively works to liberate the musician.

Set within the image of infinitely soft rain found in the closing lines of Harper's poem, Powell is removed from sensationalized, if not stereotyped, interpretations through which the pianist's music and legacy is typically viewed. Instead, Harper's Powell figure emerges from the poem virtually indistinguishable from the mode through which the poet enters his music. The Powell figure in "For Bud" articulates an expressive vision that Harper's speaker understands as shaping an expansive region of the blues continuum. In this way, he contributes to the ongoing conversation taking place between and among Black musicians within the poet's body of work. Presenting these Black artists in this way, the poet constructs an interpretive space outside and away from projections and misidentifications that, too often, inform discussions of Black expression, particularly Black music. Harper's poetic project allows Powell and many others to be seen as and for who they are and, effectively, "leave them there."

In this respect, "For Bud" presents a modal image of the pianist that is not unlike the portrait Harper renders of Miles Davis in "Alone." At the same time, the poem also enters into dialogue with the poet's other sketches of legendary musicians from the bebop era, including Charlie Parker and Billie Holiday.

Within these "jazz poems," Harper allows the mode to shape the terms by which he engages these artists and their work. In a literary project statement included with his verse in Ted Wilentz and Tom Weatherly's *Natural Process: An Anthology of New Black Poetry,* Harper writes: "my poems . . . [include] modes of perception, the relationship between ideal real and material modes of individual perception; myth, distinctions between truth and lie, the one the [sic?] patterning of particular experiences into universals" (42). Stating that his "poems are modal," the poet explains: "by modality I mean the creation of an environment to revivify and regenerate . . . and [an] environment of spirit that revitalizes man (sic) individually and culturally. . . . [Humanity] is the original *mode;* what [people] do is modal—the musicians Bud, Bird, Trane, Lady, Bessie, Pres . . . were and are all modal." To conclude his statement, Harper proclaims that "the blues singer says 'I' but the audience assumes 'We'; out of that energy becomes community and freedom. A Love Supreme" (43).

Situating his own verse within this blues-rooted conversation, Harper considers his poetic explorations of the Black music continuum. Examining his treatments of Bud Powell, Miles Davis, and other Black musicians whose work arrives in "modal" forms, the poet identifies a connection in the reciprocal, "both/and" relationship he understands as binding the "I" of the musician to the "we" of its audience. In this way, Harper maps the flow of "energy" Black music generates while cultivating the "freedom" and modal "community" that he identifies with Coltrane's notion of "a love supreme." According to German-born bassist and composer Günter H. Lenz, "poems about black [*sic*] musicians" construct the foundation of Harper's literary project. In his essay "Black Poetry and Black Music: History and Traditions: Michael Harper and John Coltrane," Lenz presents the poet's project as grounded in the blues continuum "from the beginning":"[Harper's] poems affirm the basic unity of all kinds of black [*sic*] music, yet they are not so much about 'the music' but about the personalities of the musicians, the meaning of their playing or singing as a communication of experiential reality and of triumphs over oppression and suffering" ("Black Poetry and Black Music," 295).

Lenz posits that Harper's poems written to, for, and about John Coltrane and his music make these impulses in his project fully evident: Harper's Coltrane poems "create and reveal . . . complex interrelationships" that inform the dynamic force that the poet describes as "a love supreme." According to Lenz, the poet's work in the Coltrane mode "expresses continuity, inclusiveness, complexity . . . [that] is deeply concerned with, and affected by, change" (295). He connects Harper's verse to the musician's use of and engagement with modal sensibilities: "Coltrane shows [the poet] what *modality* was as a non-western concept of life, [while illustrating what] understanding and creation means"

(294, emphasis in original). Lenz also suggests that Coltrane's musical legacy informs Harper's project by demonstrating "the power of 'both/and' instead of the Cartesian 'either/or,'" while informing its aspirations to realize a "'unity in diversity,' the 'continuum' of black [sic] culture as space . . . and as time (history/tradition) and kinship" (294). Locating these nuanced patterns within Harper's treatments of Coltrane, Lenz expands the scope of the poet's work.

While "Black Poetry and Black Music" focuses on the poet's early poetic considerations of the musician and the legacy of his work—particularly poems found in *Dear John, Dear Coltrane*—its analysis of Harper's verse is easily applied to poems from his later collections, including *Songlines in Michael-tree* and *Use Trouble*. For example, the "both/and" impulses that Lenz's essay understands as foundational to Harper's poetic portraits of Trane are helpful to reading later work, such as "A Coltrane Poem: September 23, 1998." This poem, included among the new works in *Songlines in Michaeltree,* engages Lenz's notion of "time (history/tradition) and kinship," while simultaneously serving as an example of the critic's "'continuum' of black culture as space." As such, this late-career Coltrane poem brings the musician's legacy into conversation with that of South African president Nelson Mandela. Through its nine unrhymed couplets, Harper's speaker bears witness to a temporal, spatial convergence of these two prominent twentieth-century figures within the African diaspora.

In "A Coltrane Poem: September 23, 1998," the poet recalls Mandela being awarded the Congressional Gold Medal at the United States Capitol in Washington, DC, on the sixty-second anniversary of Coltrane's birth. The poem "co-memorates" the convergence of these occasions, offering reflections on the resonance between Coltrane's revolutionary Black art and Mandela's revolutionary Black politics. The poet amplifies the magnitude of these reverberations by linking them to the day's celestial events through the poem's title. Recognizing that September 23 was the date of that year's autumnal equinox, "A Coltrane Poem" locates the day's events against a cosmic scale:

> *"Autumn Leaves"* without a bandstand
> for your vigorous arc of light
>
> though it is bright and colorful
> in the extremities of music
>
> it is no ballad or blues
> affixed to the photo album
>
> and we are not in church in fear
> of resurrection in vinyl, cd, audiosphere (365)

With these eight lines, the poet acknowledges the weight and power of the events that he is witnessing. Speaking to the cosmic, political, and aesthetic realms that have aligned before him, the poem's speaker recognizes the gravity of the moment, including its capacity for bending light and blending sound.

To capture and interpret the monumental stature of this occasion—the autumnal equinox, the Mandela award ceremony, and the anniversary of Coltrane's birth—the poet assembles a list of what "*is not*" happening, proclaiming that this "is *no* ballad or blues" and that "we are *not* in church" (emphasis added). Facilitating this transition from a set of negations to a sense of knowing, the poet shifts to a discussion of what he *actually* sees occurring, referencing Black music and Black musicians in the poem's next couplet: "and Monk is coming back to join Miles/ and Bud's 'Round Midnight' is alchemical tribute." The direction of the poem turns on these lines, as Harper's speaker invests his homage to Coltrane and Mandela with an impulse to "return" that corresponds to the notions of "equinox." Speaking "equivocally" about matters of art and politics, time and space, history and memory, all that is and isn't visible spins together, like a long-playing record, at once arriving and becoming, in sound and motion.[5]

Addressing these shifts, Harper's speaker effectively signals the arrival of a state of "evening." Acknowledging that the planet has reached a midway point in its ongoing rotation, he gestures to the possibility of realizing broader systemic change:

> "*Dear Lord*" we have been slowed in our ascension
> figurations now energies of another *spiritual*
>
> this very day Mandela spoke in the atrium
> of a would-be-government-of-the-tonalities
>
> in tribal speech as in a Babel of taxonomies
> of our earthly kingdom now original
> and not in amber at the millennium (365)

With these lines, which include italicized references to two Coltrane compositions, "Spiritual" and "Dear Lord," the poet engages "this very day." He seeks to complete his reckoning with these events and their timing, suggesting that "our earthly kingdom" is "now original / and not in amber at the millennium." Focusing on the dynamic "energies" of this moment, the poet locates its processes, consequences, and outcomes, ultimately affirming the capacity of the individual—in this case Mandela and Coltrane—to exert a vision, implement change, and serve the collective.

Assuming the blues-rooted stance in which the "I" speaks for "we" in this way, the poet concludes "A Coltrane Poem: September 23, 1998" with the words *"but of the reed, and father of the reed."* This italicized line literally and figuratively emphasizes the "both/and" posture that Lenz identifies as a principal component of Harper's Coltrane poems. Enigmatic and anti-Cartesian, the line simultaneously makes reference to (a) the basic tool Coltrane uses to produce his music (the reed) and (b) seasonal cycles of decline and renewal that occur among reeds in which the plants regenerate with the spring after drying and going to seed during the fall. Additionally, the poet's image of the reed also gestures to ancient Egypt—Africa's most recognizable empire—where the reed served as both a tool for recording events and occasions, through "the reed pen" and a spiritual ideal ("the field of reeds").

"A Coltrane Poem: September 23, 1998" maintains similarities with other Coltrane poems written late in Harper's career. Its unrhymed couplets, unadorned by punctuation, construct cadences that oscillate between poetry and prose. It is equivocal, allusive, and modal in its approach to the musician's legacy. As the final piece found in "If You Don't Force It," the second of the two sections of new work that Harper includes in *Songlines in Michaeltree*, "A Coltrane Poem: September 23, 1998" stands as both a "conclusion" and bridge to the poet's next phase of work with his Coltrane figure. Reviewing *Songlines in Michaeltree*, Jacquelyn Pope speaks to the transitional sensibilities of the volume's new verse. Comparing these poems to the more familiar, earlier works that Harper selected for this collection, Pope describes Harper's lines as "generally longer and looser" ("Citizen Pilgrim Poet," 53).

Pope supports her claim by examining another, new Coltrane poem, also composed on the anniversary of the musician's birth, "9 23 99: Coltrane Notes on the Millennium."[6] She writes that in the poem "music is an expression of both spirit and science," allowing the poet to confront the "twoness" (54) he experiences as the autumnal equinox coincides with the anniversary of Coltrane's birth. "9 23 99: Coltrane Notes" sifts and sorts the accumulation of impressions, memories, and hard facts that shape and color the poet's sense of Coltrane's composition "Alabama." This process becomes evident as the poem opens:

> "Alabama"
> no protection still
>
> that is not churchdriven
> James Weldon Johnson's alternate tune

steep archival research
in playback of the melodies

wrested in church of the beloved
(no simple timeline in melodies

hummed at the vortex of a bomb
Birmingham television hoses as carnival

reminiscent of Sharpeville)
what is African in us subliminal . . . (42)

With these lines, the poet enters into his "Coltrane mode." Working from this "both/and" state, the musician and the music become a poetic conduit for exploring memory, history, and identity within Black experience.

Throughout "Coltrane Notes," the poet pursues and marks a series of movements, creating what may be understood as a "convergent return." Harper grapples with the question of what it means to "play 'Alabama,'" just as he does in "Here Where Coltrane Is," a poem he wrote more than a quarter century earlier. Quickly and convincingly situating himself "where Coltrane is," the poet opens "Coltrane Notes" with the word "'Alabama,'" evoking the musician's response to the September 15, 1963, bombing of Birmingham, Alabama's 16th Street Baptist Church. As the poem continues, the clipped shorthand of "Coltrane Notes" serves as the poet's tool for excavating those regions of Black America that Coltrane sketches in "Alabama."

Catalyzed by this single, three-syllable word, the poem's opening lines encapsulate the sustained hostility faced by people of African descent in the United States. Conjuring images of the civil rights movement, white supremacist violence, and "the four little girls," as well as Dr. King's eulogy for them, the poet cites Coltrane's composition. Cognizant of the improvisational process that forms and informs Black music, Harper's speaker references alternative melodies Coltrane and his Quartet explored while assembling "Alabama." At the same time, extending this gloss on the idea of "alternate tunes," Harper's speaker gestures to the efforts James Weldon Johnson and his brother Rosamond made to collect spirituals and recover Black folk culture.

Along with its layered references to the Black music continuum, "Coltrane Notes" also recasts an image from "Driving the Big Chrysler across the Land of My Birth," a Coltrane poem found in Harper's *Healing Song for the Inner Ear*. He transforms a reference to innovative musician Eric Dolphy that appears in the poem from "playback of that chorus of plaints" to "playback of the melodies." Alluding to Coltrane's "Alabama" in this way, the poet engages the improvisational impulses informing his Coltrane mode. This recalibration

unleashes a cascade of images recalling the Birmingham campaign of the
Southern Christian Leadership Conference and the policing tactics—dogs,
water cannons, clubs—used against Black youth by Theophilus E. "Bull" Con-
nor, Birmingham's infamous Commissioner of Public Safety. "Coltrane Notes"
gives voice to another set of call-and-response engagements between historical
events and Black expression, effectively connecting Coltrane's "Alabama," the
Birmingham campaign, and the massacre of sixty-nine anti-apartheid demon-
strators by South African security forces in the Transvaal township of Sharpeville on March 21, 1960. Confronting similarities between apartheid-era South
Africa and Jim Crow Alabama, the poet acknowledges the international, intercontinental dimensions of legal, economic, and political inequalities within
the African Diaspora. To register these observations, Harper's speaker states,
"What is African in us subliminal" (43).

Pope states that in "Coltrane Notes on the Millennium," "the language in
this poem telegraphs events, moods, and emphases in much the same way Coltrane did in his music: breath, whether phrase or silent, is imbued with spirit"
("Citizen Pilgrim Poet," 54). Recognizing the poet's modal inflections, the critic
identifies their point of engagement with the musician's journey toward "A
Love Supreme":

> as you discovered the soprano
> which Miles saw that you had
>
> when in France the makers of instruments
> wanted to give him something   French
>
> your kiss of the fluid accents
> like no sorcerer ever heard in the vedas
>
> mistaken in byplay as prayer
> the intense registers of praise
>
> high up in the registers
> of salvation   all-knowing dross   in this world (42)

Entering territory shaped by spirituality and musical expression, the poet
moves along pathways into what Lenz calls the "'continuum' of black culture
as space" ("Black Poetry and Black Music," 294). Establishing a correlation
between the music and the mythos invested in his Coltrane figure, Harper's
speaker initiates a discussion of Black expression that works against essential-
ized notions of identity and aesthetics.

Acknowledging that a dynamic sense of "culture" informs "Coltrane
Notes," Pope explains that with this poem, "Harper expresses his conviction

that praise song focuses the mind and heart, that it can foster change, that it is the bedrock of the work toward freedom" ("Citizen Pilgrim Poet," 54). Further supporting her reading of the poem, Pope draws a quote from "Notes on Form and Fictions," Harper's postscript-project statement for *Songlines in Michael-tree*: "The world as I saw it was a cadence of songs" (42). This claim effectively underscores his exploration of the space "where Coltrane is."

Harper concludes his survey of this territory in "Coltrane Notes on the Millennium." Mapping the transcendent impulses of the musician's project, he states:

> if gnosis   is not forgiveness
> already granted in the penultimate hour
>
> (what does a black man on a foreign instrument
> have to teach the world other than intentional suffering)
>
> I would trust the pieta as parlance
> in the free gift faithfully offered
>
> as your compositions
> transcribed yet unrecorded
>
> in the rigor of a practice session
> as the reed enables the passage of praise
>
> all technical mastery
> layed at the feet   of the high mode (43)

The poem ends with these lines, with the poet accessing Coltrane's "high mode." Harper's speaker creates a literary bulwark against the formal power that Lenz describes in his essay as the "Cartesian 'either/or.'" The final six couplets of "Coltrane Notes on the Millennium" illustrate the fluid ethos the poet invests in his Coltrane figure, identifying Coltrane as a "black man" while bringing him into conversation with "gnosis" and "the pieta," intellectual and aesthetic concepts embedded in Western sensibilities and traditions. As he engages these impulses, Harper's speaker renders another improvisational "alternate" take on a line from "Driving the Big Chrysler,"[7] parenthetically asking: "what does a black man on a foreign instrument / have to teach the world other than intentional suffering."

Performing this series of translations, code switches, and improvisational shifts, the poet underlines the core of his poetic project. In "Coltrane Notes on the Millennium," Harper's speaker incorporates a "both/and" dynamic into his praise for Coltrane. He does so, acknowledging the musician's engagement with oral/aural tradition ("your compositions / transcribed yet unrecorded"), along

with his commitment to preparation ("rigor of a practice session") and dedication to performed excellence ("all technical mastery"). In this way, the poem
effectively speaks back to Lenz's reading of Harper's Coltrane poems from
"Black Poetry and Black Music," where the critic writes, "Coltrane's *music*
provides *images* of process strong enough to energize the poet" (301, emphasis
in original).

Speaking to the exchange he observes taking place between poem, poet,
and Coltrane's music, Lenz effectively identifies their shared pursuit of "A Love
Supreme." The critic expands his examination of Harper's Coltrane mode,
bringing attention to the poet's broader claims for Black music. Lenz draws a
passage from the liner notes Harper wrote for *John Coltrane,* a Prestige double
album reissue of Coltrane's sessions with pianist Red Garland. The critic
quotes Harper's description of Black music as a "continuous process of fluid-
ity in the passes of creation, human creation, contingent human experience,
ancestral reality, black history, [and] aesthetic vision" ("Black Poetry and Black
Music," 301).

By bringing this approach to Harper's work with the Coltrane legacy, Lenz
establishes a critical pathway for discussing another late-career poetic treatment of the musician and his work, "The Book on Trane." In this poem from
Use Trouble, Harper once again proceeds along a route of "return," locating
Coltrane in the "Alabama" composition:

> In "Alabama" an off version of spiritual
> J. Rosamond Johnson's hymnal holdovers
>
> from his brother's gatherings in the field
> James Weldon Johnson not allowed to beckon
>
> his students into his Fisk 'sitting room'
> because his wife has covered the furnishings
>
> so JWJ stood at the fence in Nashville
> talking to his children in creative writing class (216)

Using a series of unpunctuated, unrhymed couplets, "The Book on Train"
connects Coltrane's composition commemorating the September 15, 1963,
bombing of Birmingham's Sixteenth Street Baptist Church to the Black folklore
collection and recovery efforts that James Weldon Johnson and his brother,
J. Rosamond Johnson, conducted while producing *The Book of American
Negro Spirituals.*

Enacting "generative kinship" and engaging "convergent history," the first
four couplets of "The Book on Train" undertake a "return" to "Alabama," Coltrane, and the Johnson brothers. Harper's speaker gestures to underexamined

connections linking Coltrane's music to the Johnsons's project, as he does in "9 23 99: Coltrane Notes on the Millennium." The poet references an alternative melody for the spiritual "Nobody Knows the Trouble I've Seen," collected by J. Rosamond Johnson, which served as a source of inspiration for Coltrane's composition, "Spiritual." Having established these connections, Harper's speaker explores the boundaries of complicated identity rituals involving class, geography, and color that ultimately counteract efforts to "uplift" rank-and-file Black people. The contradictions invested in these limits become evident in the poem as Johnson is "not allowed to beckon / his students into his Fisk 'sitting room'" at the same time the poet seems to nod at Johnson's improvisational response to these exclusionary practices in the line, "JWJ stood at the fence in Nashville."

Yet as the poem continues, Harper's speaker praises "JWJ" and the actions he coordinated in his roles of as educator, activist, and artist, despite internal divisions he identifies within Black America. The scope and scale of the "both/ and" approach that Johnson brought to his efforts to counteract the corrosive influence of white supremacy become evident:

> ex-slaves accommodating only the highest plane of service
> refusing segregation as supremacist covenant
>
> enacted to prohibit any development
> except the group areas acts (in the fields) (216)

Once again, Harper's speaker deploys Coltrane and his musical project to initiate an intercontinental, cross-cultural discussion concerning the lives and living conditions of Black people throughout the African Diaspora. In "The Book on Trane," the poet extends the comparison he makes elsewhere, bringing American-style, Jim Crow segregation into conversation with the Union of South Africa's Group Areas Act of 1950. Again, with Coltrane's "Alabama" serving as a modal refrain within "The Book on Trane," Harper's speaker revisits links between James Weldon Johnson and the musician as well as ties binding Birmingham to Sharpeville, which he also treats in "9 23 99: Coltrane Notes on the Millennium."

With Coltrane's music serving as a poetic conduit of "return" in "The Book on Trane," Harper's poem concludes with a "silent" invocation of the musician and his legacy. Throughout the course of the poem, the poet assembles layers of imagery, consolidating links between his literary project, the musician's legacy, and Black expressive tradition. Accessing the Coltrane mode in this way, Harper's speaker constructs a bridge between the spiritual, aesthetic, and physical dimensions of Coltrane's life and music:

> yet he has built a church on these vestments
> passageway etched in exquisite pain
>
> only tone remembers   a scale untended
> by the best technicians without the beloved's kiss
>
> the vessel of song is the spiritual
> the essence of singing the spirit itself "a love supreme" (216)

In the closing couplets of "The Book on Trane," the poet traces Coltrane's movements through the spirituals, entering interior regions of the Black music continuum. Attending to the music's "tone" and "scale," he locates the confluence of kinship and history where the musician "built a church" from "these vestments." Identifying "the spiritual" as Coltrane's "vessel of song," Harper's speaker completes his efforts to recollect, re-enter, and return the musician's vision of "'a love supreme.'"

With "The Book on Trane" becoming one more chorus in the extended song line comprising the poet's Coltrane mode, it finds resonance with another set of early Coltrane poems that the poet includes in "My Book on Trane," the fourth section of *Healing Song for the Inner Ear*. Beyond their titular similarities, this series of eleven, lesser- known poetic examinations of John Coltrane by Michael S. Harper speaks to "The Book on Train" through its discussion of the musician's career and his artistic legacy. Arriving in a blend of written genres that includes "poetry," "memoir," and "journalism," this series of eye- and ear-witness accounts sketches Coltrane on and away from the bandstand. Poems included in "My Book on Trane" enter the poet's longer, larger discussion concerning the musician and his body of work, creating an intersecting set of literary portraits in which Coltrane and his music speak to and through Harper's poetic vision.

Poems from the "My Book on Trane" sequence, such as "Bandstand" and "Obscurity," consider the musician and his artistic project as simultaneously sustaining and being sustained by the complex, blues-rooted networks that undergird Black culture and its traditions. At the same time, other work from "My Book on Train"—including "Arpeggios," "Solo," and "Polls"—address evolving existential and political realities confronting mid-twentieth-century Black America, including Black musicians. Harper's poetic series explores the underlying contributions that John Coltrane makes to Black expressive tradition. As Günter Lenz suggests in "Black Poetry and Black Music," the poet "has succeeded in working out in his poetry . . . [a] 'vision of liberation' of perception and sensibility and of 'community and freedom' which he experienced in Coltrane's music" (314). The poet identifies Coltrane and his music as contributing to Black America's political and social dialogue in the mid-twentieth century.

Ultimately, poems from Harper's "My Book on Trane" sequence distinguish the musician and his body of work from the legend that envelops him and his music. This set of impressionistic portraits depicts Coltrane and his musical cohort in deep, contextualized relief. For example, in the cycle's eighth poem, "Rumors," Harper focuses on a violent, 1956 confrontation between Coltrane and Miles Davis. Foreshadowing the dissolution of the musician's professional relationship with Davis and the intensification of his desire to extend the limits of his performance, the poet writes: "When Miles smacked your face / for playing the right notes; / after the encounter, your solos / paralyzed the audience" (74). This pattern also emerges from the sequence's title poem, "My Book on Trane." In this poem, for example, Harper captures the intensity Elvin Jones brought to his sessions with Trane, conjuring an image of the drummer entering the club with "the smoke coming off Elvin / as he strides across the street" (78). Similarly, in "Polls," the poet examines the American music industry, acknowledging critical misreadings that Coltrane's trailblazing musical work received from certain critics and audiences. In so doing, the poet effectively surveys the aesthetics and politics of the color line: "Some bloods can't count and won't vote; / imagine Desmond ahead of Trane / on the wrong instrument" (69).

The poet delivers another thick description of Coltrane's experiments with sound and performance through the "My Book on Train" sequence in "Sugarloaf":

> At the bridge Chambers would stop
> humming in the high registers,
> Philly Joe in the outhouse
> kicking his traps,
> one last exit blocked for Garland,
> out-of-doors in block chords,
> trying to double-clutch and catch up,
> giving the finger to engineers. (75)

The dense, layered imagery in "Sugarloaf" and other poems from *Healing Song* was received enthusiastically. At the time of the volume's publication, critics praised the poet for his work's engagement with Black music. For example, writing for *American Poetry Review*, J. R. Payne suggests that "like contemporary jazz, Harper's language is so compressed it gives a diamond light, illuminating many precious traditions in a fresh mellow glow" (Payne, "Review of *Healing Song for the Inner Ear*," 117). Similarly, Frank Allen describes the verse in *Healing Song* as "woven of a jazz idiom, outrage at social injustice, and personal retrospection," before calling the volume "a free-flowing panoramic view of Harper's varied career teaching and traveling, Black music and black folktales, grown out of African anguish and jim crow [*sic*] inequities" (Allen, Review of *Healing Song for the Inner Ear,* 2284).

Shortly before *Healing Song* was published, Harper was interviewed by David Lloyd for *TriQuarterly.* During their conversation, Lloyd asked the poet for his thoughts about the poetry market in the United States. Harper explained that "[he'd] spent a lot of time not reacting to whatever the market demanded" before saying that he was "asked to write a biography of Coltrane" by "people who wanted to get some insight into Coltrane's private life." Demonstrating his skepticism about this type of market driven project, the poet explains that he declined the offer because he "didn't think it was anybody's business" ("Interview with Michael S. Harper," 122). He explained that the "reason [for] writing ["Dear John, Dear Coltrane"], retrospectively, is very different from what it was people thought the poem was about [at the time of its publication]." Harper goes on to say that he "point[s] out to people that [aspects of the poem] had been a tradition among black [*sic*] Americans for many years now," adding that "the poem doesn't come out of a vacuum" (122).

As the poet's first collection of new work in a decade, *Healing Song for the Inner Ear* was both highly anticipated and warmly received. The poems were longer and, for some readers, perhaps more "difficult" as the poet brought a more experimental approach to familiar subjects. The collection speaks to the elevated status and visibility that Harper gained from his first six volumes of verse, which clearly established him as a fixture on the American literary landscape. Whether he was contributing to or editing high-profile journals, reading on the poetry circuit, or participating in international events sponsored by the US Department of State, Harper had become a notable voice in American letters. In addition to participating in these activities, he served the needs of Brown University's English Department by teaching, advising, and working with graduate students as well as directing its Creative Writing Program.[8] He contributed to several publications that brought attention to the literary work of Black writers from earlier generations, including Robert Hayden, Ralph Ellison, and Sterling A. Brown.

It is not surprising that from 1975 through *Healing Song*'s publication in 1985, Harper's rate of poetic production slowed dramatically. After having published six volumes of verse in seven years, Harper embraced his efforts as curator and conservator of Black letters. Pursuing his duties as "cultural custodian," Harper worked to promote and preserve the literary legacies of Hayden, Ellison, and Brown. He was instrumental in Hayden's efforts to complete

American Journal,[9] a volume which includes several of Hayden's masterworks, including "A Letter from Phillis Wheatley," "Paul Laurence Dunbar," and the volume's title poem "[American Journal]."[10] Following Hayden's death in February 1980, Harper edited a special issue of *Obsidian,* dedicated to the poet's legacy. Harper also served as a champion for Sterling A. Brown, keeping this elder poet in the public eye and his writing in print. He edited *The Collected Poems of Sterling A. Brown* (1980) and, along with Robert Stepto, managed Brown's schedule of poetry readings, including the tour of northeastern college campuses that brought the poet to Williams College, his alma mater, for the first time in fifty years.

Harper and Stepto published Brown's remarks at Williams College as "A Son's Return: 'Oh, Didn't He Ramble," in *Chant of Saints: A Gathering of Afro-American Literature, Art, and Scholarship.* This innovative interdisciplinary, multigenre anthology of Black literature and culture stands as the largest custodial undertaking of Harper's career between 1976 and 1986. The volume, coedited with Robert Stepto, connects poetry, fiction, and literary theory with Black studies scholarship and history. Looking to shift the focus of debates that shaped Black letters following the Black Arts Movement, *Chant of Saints* brings work by Black writers, such as Ralph Ellison, Toni Morrison, Gayl Jones, and Derek Walcott, into conversation with essays by Robert Ferris Thompson, Melvin Dixon, Sherley Anne Williams, and Alice Walker.

Working with Stepto on the *Chant of Saints* anthology brought Harper into contact with Ellison. The warm relationship that followed allowed Harper to organize the "Celebrating Ralph Ellison Festival" at Brown University in September 1979. This two-day event featured a symposium on *Invisible Man* and included an unveiling ceremony in which a portrait of Inman Page—the first person of African descent to graduate from Brown—was put on permanent display at the Rockefeller Library.[11] Scholarly and creative work presented at the festival appeared in a special issue of the *Carleton Miscellany.* Harper coedited this volume with John Wright. It includes the keynote address "Going to the Territory," which Ellison delivered during the festival. This talk was later published as the title piece of *Going to the Territory,* the final collection that Ellison published in his lifetime.

Harper's poetic project gains a measure of critical context when the verse he includes in *Healing Song for the Inner Ear* is read while keeping in mind his custodial efforts and the interview with Lloyd. His conversation with the critic provides insight into poems from "Peace on Earth," the final section of the *Healing Song* volume. Harper expresses his sense that the Coltrane figure and his "Coltrane Poems" advance individual and collective aesthetic and spiritual exploration. In this way, when Harper's poems from "Peace on Earth" engage verse from "My Book on Trane," they configure a new set of connections linking Coltrane's musical legacy and Harper's body of work.

Throughout the course of the three "autobiographical" Coltrane poems that comprise "Peace on Earth," Harper's speaker effectively channels the musician's thoughts and perspectives. The poet provides the musician with an opportunity to "speak for himself." As such, the three-pieces of this poetic "autobiography"—"A Narrative of the Life and Times of John Coltrane: Played by Himself," "Driving the Big Chrysler across the Country of My Birth," and the section's title poem, "Peace on Earth"—illustrate the poet's sustained explorations of kinship and history through Black music. This project becomes evident as "A Narrative of the Life and Times of John Coltrane" brings the Coltrane legacy into conversation with two foundational elements of Black experience in the United States: the slave narrative and the Great Migration.

These two topics emerge at the outset of "A Narrative of the Life and Times of John Coltrane: Played by Himself," as the poem's title and its epigraph riff on autobiographical works produced by early Black writers, referred to as "slave narratives."[12] As such, the poem's title clearly speaks to both Fredrick Douglass's *Narrative of the Life of Frederick Douglass, An American Slave, Written by Himself* and Harriet Jacobs's *Incidents in the Life of a Slave Girl. Written by Herself*. At the same time, the poem extends its engagement with Black experience in the United States by referencing Coltrane's birthplace in its epigraph, "Hamlet, North Carolina" and by mapping Coltrane's movement from "South to North. " In this way, the poem simultaneously further aligns the musician with Douglass and Jacobs while effectively linking Harper's Coltrane figure to the Great Migration.

Framed in this way, the Coltrane figure in "Narrative in the Life and Times of John Coltrane" moves North in a search for greater aesthetic and expressive freedom. He explores possibilities that arrive as he traces the trajectory of Coltrane's life and career, "as played by himself." For example, in the third stanza, presenting Coltrane's musical development as occurring in four distinct phases, the poet writes "a capella notes on our church choir / doping me into arpeggios, / into *sheets of sound* labeling me / into dissonance" (92, emphasis in original). Harper's speaker charts the arc of the musician's development, accounting for changes in his playing styles and compositional patterns, from his days as a church choir member through his time leading experimental ensembles. As the poem continues, Harper's speaker extends this project, identifying Coltrane's moment of aesthetic awakening in the poem's fifth stanza:

> one night I was playing with Bostic,
> blacking out, coming alive only to melodies
> when I could play my parts:
> And then, on a train to Philly,
> I sang "Naima" locking the doors
> without exit no matter what song
> I sang (93)

Gesturing to the musician's battles with drug and alcohol addiction and his days with Earl Bostic's big band, these lines reference the title of Coltrane's 1959 composition, "Naima," that Coltrane dedicated to his first wife. The poet marks a succession of personal transformations that enabled a sideman, prone to "blacking out," to become a virtuoso, bandleader, and composer, capable of "locking the door/ without exit no matter what song."

With these lines, Harper's Coltrane mode moves into action, conveying the speaker's desire to evolve and improve, not only with respect to his musical understanding and execution, but also in terms of his personal and artistic development. The poem concludes with the poet acknowledging the "both / and" impulses informing these ambitions. As "A Narrative of the Life and Times of John Coltrane" closes, the speaker announces: "I broke loose from crystalline habits / I thought would bring me that sound" (93). As the Coltrane figure emancipates himself, synchronizing his physical and spiritual needs, he also realizes his aesthetic ambitions. By undergoing these transitions, the poem comes to serve as a prologue for the "Peace on Earth" sequence's second poem, "Driving the Big Chrysler across the Country of My Birth."

With the Coltrane figure's transformation process taking place, "Driving the Big Chrysler" begins as he articulates his broader vision, greater foresight, and expanded range of motion. These abilities allow the poet to navigate and narrate his speaker's transcontinental musical odyssey. The Coltrane figure arrives, liberated from historical burdens embedded in Black America's North/South geographic axis. Removed from underground railroads, Great Migrations, and visions of a "free North," Harper's speaker travels from east to west in this poem, accompanied by members of his "Classic Quartet." Drummer Elvin Jones, pianist McCoy Tyner, and bassist Jimmy Garrison join Harper's Coltrane figure in "Driving the Big Chrysler," seeking new possibilities and enhanced personal and artistic freedom as they embark upon their voyage.

The expedition begins in the borough of Queens, New York, quickly moving west toward the Allegheny Mountains, passing through the tunnels on the Pennsylvania Turnpike. The speaker offers observations on Detroit and

Wyoming, before arriving on the West Coast in Oakland and Los Angeles. Throughout the journey, the Coltrane figure and his collaborators travel as Black men and musicians. They survey, collect, and confirm abiding connections that they maintain with "the country of their birth." As such, "Driving the Big Chrysler" becomes a trek through space, time, and musical experimentation, effectively confirming the Quartet's status as trailblazers and pioneering musicians. Tracking the progress of its Coltrane figure in "elk-miles," the poem traverses vast stretches of the American landscape. "Truck tires" and "bus terminal[s]" become transfer points for their expedition and its aesthetic experiments. Harper's speaker sings a song of the open road, capturing its ephemera and recording its permanent features.

Continuing his westward movement, the Coltrane figure also sings America, reanimating and reimagining mythologies invested in this land as births and belongings. The Big Chrysler facilitates these transitions as the poem's speaker transports Black voices, Black figures, and Black music to new frontiers. For example, in the poem's fourth stanza, Harper's speaker drives his "sunship from Motown" into a "Wyoming sunset." Performing acts of reclamation as he moves across the American landscape in this way, the Coltrane figure effectively delivers a set of variations on the "memories and modal songs" that the poet assembles in "Here Where Coltrane Is."

"Driving the Big Chrysler" initiates a journey in which the trope of "return" once again serves the poet's literary consideration of the Coltrane legacy. For example, through the course of the poem, Harper "returns" to images of Coltrane's musical collaborators, including Eric Dolphy, Thelonious Monk, and McCoy Tyner. This Coltrane figure also "returns" to a list of compositions—"Round Midnight," "Woodn't You," and "The Promise"— that arrives "embossed against the memo stand" above the western horizon. "Driving the Big Chrysler" also includes specific sites of return, such as "Camarillo," where the Coltrane figure makes connections with "the life and times" of Charlie "Bird" Parker.[13]

Harper's speaker records a series of specific sites that he encounters while moving "across the country of his birth." Identifying the particular sense of energy and power that he experiences on this journey, the poem opens with Harper's Coltrane figure describing the anticipation that he feels while at the wheel of "the Big Chrysler." At the opening of the poem he states, "I would wait for the tunnels / to glide into overdrive," before going on to situate himself within portions of an American landscape that is, at once, formed and informed by Black music and Black experience. These circumstances arrive clearly in the third stanza of Harper's poem, where the speaker delivers a meditation on saxophonist Lester Young:

> I thought of Lester
> Chinese face on a Christmas
> Card mailed to my home in Queens: Prez!
> I saw him cry in joy as the recordings
> Bird memorized in Missouri breaks
> floated in Bessie's floodless hill:
> *Backwater Blues:* I could never play
> such sweetness again: Lady said Prez
> was the closest she ever got to real
> escort, him worrying who was behind
> him in arcades memorizing his tunes. (Harper 94)

With these lines the Coltrane figure performs an excavation project that moves through layers of history and kinship, revealing the bedrock of Black musical tradition. In this acknowledgment of his aesthetic forbearers—Lester Young ("Prez"), Charlie Parker ("Bird"), Bessie Smith, and Billie Holiday ("Lady")—Harper's speaker delivers an appreciation of these musicians' and their explorations of melody, rhythm, and harmonics. Recognizing that their movements through these expressive regions made his project possible, the speaker offers an account of the travels he's embarked upon, along with members of his Quartet. Accounting for their progress, both collectively and as individuals, he recognizes that his group has moved beyond the aesthetic boundaries established by their swing and bebop ancestors. Addressing kinship in these terms, the Coltrane figure almost regretfully explains that the Big Chrysler, fueled by modal impulses and improvisation, has taken him to a place where he "could never play such sweetness again."

In the poem's fourth stanza, Harper's speaker continues to appreciate the distances he and members of his Quartet have traveled on their journeys of discovery. Musing that "I thought of how many tunes / I'd forgotten in my suspensions of the pentatonic scale," he contemplates tradition, form, and technical mastery. Ultimately, the Coltrane figure acknowledges that he has not been unchanged by the journey: "I can never write a bar of this music / in this life chanting toward paradise" (95). However, "paradise" is not the final destination for Harper's exploration of the Coltrane mode. The musician returns as the speaker of "Peace on Earth," the third and final poem in the sequence of autobiographical Coltrane poems from *Healing Song.*

This poem's title refers to a composition—"Peace on Earth"—that Coltrane performed during the 1966 tour of Japan with his "Final Quartet," the ensemble that included Alice Coltrane (piano), Pharoah Sanders (bass clarinet/ saxophone), Jimmy Garrison (bass), and Rashied Ali (drums). "Peace on

Earth," like "Driving the Big Chrysler," identifies Harper's Coltrane figure
as being on the move, taking his music beyond conventional limits and claiming space outside of the geographic and aesthetic boundaries associated with
blues-rooted modes of expression. The poem begins:

> Tunes come to me at morning
> prayer, after flax sunflower
> seeds jammed into a coffee can. (96)

Here, the Coltrane figure is a way from the bandstand, the club, or the concert
hall. He is in daylight and arrives as a seeker, willing himself to become "at
peace on earth." Addressing the possibilities that are evident to him, Harper's
speaker asserts that "my music's / voice of praise to our oneness" (96) effectively demonstrating "where Coltrane is."

Discussing "Peace on Earth" in "Black Poetry and Black Music," Günter
Lenz explains that the poem "pursues the religious, the spiritual meaning of
Coltrane's playing" (314). His reading of the poem is confirmed as the poet's
speaker makes reference to Coltrane compositions such as "Spiritual" and
"Reverend King." Kimberly W. Benston also brings attention to the elevated
spiritual and aesthetic awareness that defined the musician's later works in his
essay "Late Coltrane: A Re-Membering of Orpheus," where Benston quotes
Coltrane as saying: "My goal in meditating on the unity of life through music
always remains the same. And that is to uplift people as much as I can. To
inspire them to realize more and more of their capacities for living meaningful
lives" (Harper and Stepto, *Chant of Saints*, 424). "Peace on Earth" connects
with these impulses as the poem's Coltrane figure recalls his visit to Japan:

> I prayed at the shrine
> for the war dead broken
> at Nagasaki;
>
> the tears on the lip of my soprano
> glistened in the sun. (96)

The speaker allows his music to stand as a medium of reconciliation and acknowledgment. He speaks to notions of sacrifice and sustained tradition, explaining that there is "no high as intense as possessions / given up in practice"
and presenting "Syeeda's 'Song Flute' charts / my playing for the ancestors"
(97). Aligning his vision of the Coltrane mode with his own poetic project in
this way, Harper's speaker allows the musician's legacy to access the ancestral
and historical networks that both artists understand as informing all modes of
Black expression, including Black music.

"Peace on Earth" reaches its conclusion as the Coltrane figure continues to expand the frontiers of blues-rooted expression. Gesturing to its power, magnitude, and possibilities, Harper's speaker addresses the cosmic scale of this project:

> how could I do otherwise,
> passing so quickly in this galaxy
>
> there is no time for being
>
> to be paid in Acknowledgment;
> all praise to the phrase brought to me:
> salaams of becoming:
> A LOVE SUPREME: (97)

Having reached an expressive and existential tipping point—at once, a "return" and "no return"—the Coltrane figure, arriving with "salaams of becoming," reverently declares this state to be "A LOVE SUPREME." This poem completes the three-poem "autobiographical" sequence and its consideration of the Coltrane legacy. Addressing the aspirational, aesthetic, and spiritual aspects of the musician's work, Harper pursues pathways and avenues that Coltrane traveled as an innovative Black artist and pioneering improvisational musician.

When Harper's speaker concludes "Peace on Earth" by proclaiming "A LOVE SUPREME," this mid-career Coltrane poem connects with "Dear John, Dear Coltrane," the title piece from Harper's first collection of verse. The two poems come into conversation, recalling that "Dear John, Dear Coltrane" opens with an epigraph that repeats "*a love supreme*" four times in italics. The phrase ultimately becomes a cornerstone of the work, as it appears at five distinct moments throughout the poem. It punctuates the bold, even provocative, gloss on the musician's "life and times" conveyed by the poet in "Dear John, Dear Coltrane." In "Map of the Soothsayer," Herman Beavers discusses Harper's exploration of the Coltrane mode, explaining that "Coltrane's technique offered Harper a window into how history could echo through all we do and see" (148). Beavers suggests that pursuing this technique "demanded an innovative posture, demanded that the poet eschew the role of troubadour to become a soothsayer of the highest rank" (148).

Treating Harper's engagement with the Coltrane mode from this perspective, "Dear John, Dear Coltrane" stands as a distinct type of poetic premonition. As "soothsayer," Harper's speaker foresees the musician's decline and demise. Death and dismemberment haunts and hunts the Coltrane figure throughout the poem. In its opening lines, the poet couples Coltrane—both as a Black man and a Black artist—with the enduring specter of American white supremacist violence: "Sex fingers toes/ in the marketplace/ near your father's church /in Hamlet, North Carolina" (74). With the music serving as Coltrane's best mode of resistance and principal means of response, the poet witnesses the musician "move/ by river, through the swamps, / singing: *a love supreme, a love supreme*" before he elects to "pick up the horn/with some will and blow/ into the freezing night *a love supreme, a love supreme* (74).

Despite these efforts to elude and escape pursuit—either by entering "the electric city" or playing his "song now crystal /and the blues"—Harper's Coltrane figure cannot stave off the inevitable outcomes meted out by this hostile environment. These conditions become fully evident in the poem's closing stanza:

> So sick
> you couldn't play *Naima*
> so flat we ached
> for song you'd concealed
> with your own blood,
> your diseased liver gave
> out its purity,
> the inflated heart
> pumps out, the tenor kiss,
> tenor love:
> *a love supreme, a love supreme—*
> *a love supreme, a love supreme* (75)

"Dear John, Dear Coltrane" leaves no chance for return; the speaker's rendezvous with "tenor kiss" and "tenor love" are both destined to resolve with or through his death. Although the poem was published approximately three years after the musician died in 1967, in Harper's interview with David Lloyd he clearly exhibits what Beavers calls the "innovative posture" of the soothsayer: "I wrote the poem . . . before [Coltrane] died" (Lloyd, "Interview with Michael S. Harper," 122).

Poem and poet effectively imagine the Coltrane figure as both an accomplished artist, capable of realizing the transcendence of "a love supreme," and a Black man in the United States, vulnerable to the nation's voracious and insatiable appetite for Black bodies. The poem thereby becomes a grim epistolary elegy. This impulse begins with the first four lines, where the poet invites discussion of the manner by which white lynch mobs collected trophies from the bodies of Black victims.[14] Similarly, the poem's title also speaks to the "twoness" of both John Coltrane, the man, and John Coltrane, the artist. "Dear John, Dear Coltrane" simultaneously traces the movements of these figures: "John" and

"Coltrane." In both cases, Harper's Coltrane figure(s) follow a line(s) of flight that recalls people of African descent, escaping from slave catchers, moving "by river through the swamps." At the same time Harper's "John | Coltrane" seeks a freedom that he imagines as "the electric city," where the figure arrives as both fugitive and refugee.

The second stanza of "Dear John, Dear Coltrane" opens and the Coltrane figure, once again, experiences a form of embodied peril: "Dawn comes and you cook / up the thick sin 'tween / impotence and death" (74). Gesturing toward the musician's struggles with substance abuse and addiction, the poet recognizes the dangerous and ultimately debilitating impact that drugs and alcohol had on Coltrane. The musician's triumph in his battles with narcotics becomes "fuel" for both the poem and Coltrane's artistic process. As such, the musician and his "tenor sax cannibal / heart" work to release "genitals and sweat / that make you clean." This alchemical process provides Harper's Coltrane with a reprieve and a sense of clarity, expressed and explored by the poet through the chant of "love supreme." In his essay "Michael Harper's Extended Tree: John Coltrane and Sterling Brown," Robert Stepto discusses the repeated use of the chant in "Dear John, Dear Coltrane." He suggests that the poem's mellow, hypnotic refrain—"a love supreme, a love supreme"—is not a gratuitous gesture to this well-known Coltrane composition and chant. Instead, Stepto like Beavers understands it as a "revealing prophetic vision and wholeness, generating an inner power which one can sustain personal and cultural—immediate and historical—assault" (Stepto, "Michael Harper's Extended Tree," 5).

Charting a course of doubled resistance and double pursuance, Harper's "Dear John, Dear Coltrane" simultaneously forms and defines the modal engagement his body of work maintains with Black music. Realizing the resistant, allusive ethos of "a love supreme," the poem locates the enigmatic transcendence that the poet finds in the muted blues of Miles Davis ("I'll leave him there") and the dominant left hand he associates with Bud Powell ("sweetest left hook you / ever dug, baby"). The poet honors blues-rooted musical expression, especially when it arrives in the form of jazz. With the music's impulses directing and sustaining his body of work, they contextualize and sustain Harper's sense of both generative kinship and convergent history. His vision and poetic project are informed by a collective legacy founded by Charlie Parker, Billie Holiday, Coleman Hawkins, Bessie Smith, and Dexter Gordon, to name a few of his aesthetic ancestors. It is, however, the music of John Coltrane that ultimately allows Harper to discover the full extent of his work's expressive possibilities.

The poet demonstrates a foundational awareness of his poetry's engagement with the Coltrane legacy, particularly the sonic experiments that the

musician conducted with his "Classic Quartet" in his interview with Edward
Hirsch. This becomes evident as the poet states that listening to the ensemble's
music "just opened up all kinds of things to me and I decided that there were
ritual elements in the integration of rights which needed to be put into certain
things I was interested in. . . . It seems to me that one of the reasons why artists
make art is to create force" (Hirsch, "An Interview with Michael S. Harper,"
11). He ultimately arrives at his reckoning with this "force" in the third stanza
of "Dear John, Dear Coltrane." Delivering a sobering, direct, and rhetori-
cally diffident sketch of the musician through question-and-answer, call-and-
response dialogue, Harper writes,

> *Why you so black?*
> *cause I am*
> *why you so funky?*
> *cause I am*
> *why you so black?*
> *cause I am*
> *why you so sweet?*
> *cause I am*
> *why you so black?*
> *cause I am*
> *a love supreme, a love supreme:* (75)

These lines echo the repetition and difference that Harper affirms and asserts
in "Brother John," the first poem in the *Dear John, Dear Coltrane* collection.
In "Brother John," the poet similarly presents Blackness as identity, repeatedly
stating, "Black man / I'm a black man; I'm a black; I am." However, throughout his similarly repetitious passage from "Dear John, Dear Coltrane, the poet
implores readers to enter, search, and pursue the expansive reaches of both
the Black music continuum and the Coltrane mode, as written by Michael S.
Harper.

CHAPTER 5

Psalm (Memory and Remembrances)

Michael S. Harper demonstrates his well-defined interests in Black experience and American expressive traditions throughout his body of poetic work. In "Office Hours: A Memoir and an Interview with Michael S. Harper," Heather Treseler engages the poet in a discussion about his verse and reflects on his project. At one point in their wide-ranging conversation, Harper describes himself as "an initiate of the *subjective correlative.*" When prompted by Treseler to say more about this aspect of his work, the poet explains that by using the phrase he is "going directly in the teeth of [T. S.] Eliot" ("Office Hours," 120). Suggesting that his work seeks to turn tables on Eliot's notion of the objective correlative, Harper states: "I think [Eliot] was wrong on many things, including race and how to read canonical texts." His own sense of poetics is "tied to the notion of exegesis of explication," which he sees as indicating "something about the ways in which a poem can be structured" (121). Harper concludes his thoughts on "the subjective correlative" and its impact within his poetic project: "When I take risks in the public domain, I am trying to expand the dialogue by using references to sacred books which are not English or American" (122).

Within this portion of his interview with Treseler, Harper brings insight into his project as a whole. In particular, describing his efforts to "expand the dialogue" by referencing "sacred books, which are not English or American," the poet effectively brings his body of work into conversation with John Coltrane's composition "Psalm," the fourth and final movement of his suite, "A Love Supreme." Recognizing the esteemed position that Coltrane and his music maintain within Harper's project underscores this connection. Identifying the imprint that both "A Love Supreme" (the composition) and "a love supreme" (the concept) have made on the poet's verse amplifies these links.

These connections become evident in the poet's quote about "sacred books" as gesturing to the Hebrew Bible and Coltrane's "Psalm" as being aligned with both "the psalm" as a poetic mode and "Psalms" as biblical texts. With these points of convergence simultaneously linking its literary, expressive, and spiritual ambitions, Harper's verse moves to "expand the dialogue" in what the poet calls "the public domain" by pursuing what he recognizes as "a love supreme."

In "Psalm and Anti-Psalm: A Personal View," Alicia Ostriker provides a critical framework for understanding Harper's explorations of these territories. Ostriker's essay brings the Psalms into a dialogue with the "both/and" sensibility that informs Harper's poetic project. She writes: "the Psalms are glorious. No, the Psalms are terrible. No, the Psalms are both glorious and terrible. Both attractive and repulsive to me emotionally and theologically. I read as a poet and a woman . . . and when I read these poems, I experience a split-screen effect: wildly contradictory responses" (11). Describing the Psalms as "the poetry of emotional turbulence," Ostriker asserts that they are at once "uncontrollable and unpredictable." She suggests that "the emotions of the Psalms surge and collapse like breaking waves," capable of delivering "joy and despair and hope and frustration and fear and anger and grief and sorrow" (11). As such, the Psalms arrive as an irregular, even contradictory, mode.

Ostriker asserts that "the Psalms are the prototype in English devotional poetry and possibly of lyric poetry in general" (13). Written in the summer of 2002, the essay reads the Psalms as an emotional and poetic backdrop for the 9/11 attacks of 2001. As such, Ostriker uses the Psalms to address what was, at the time of the essay's publication, a very fresh wound. She describes hearing the psalmist's voice engage celebration, commemoration, remembrance, and lament. At the same time, Ostriker also maintains that all too often, theologians and literary critics conveniently select passages from specific Psalms to suit their claims. Careful to avoid this temptation, she considers whole works, embracing their complexities and contradictions. Ostriker's treatment of the Psalms finds multiple points of intersection with Harper's body of work.

In Treseler's "Office Hours," Harper discusses the power of poetic multivocality in a way that resembles Ostriker's approach to the Psalms. The poet explains that "there are things like 'voicings' . . . *where one is always responsible for the speaker,*" before he reminds Treseler that "the speakers are allowed to vary" (120, emphasis in original). Harper follows the type of variegated, even divergent, pathways that Ostriker identifies in the Psalms, recognizing these "voicings" as animating those "sacred books which are not English or American." Harper pursues these impulses in a seven-line poem entitled "Psalm." The poem initially appeared in *Songlines in Michaeltree,* serving as the epigraph for the collection's in-memoriam dedication to the poet's mother,

Katherine Johnson Harper. "Psalm" also appears in *I Do Believe in People: Re-membrances of W. Warren Harper 1915–2004,* a limited-edition volume Harper dedicated to his late father's memory. In this collection, the poem is found on the overleaf of a pullout depiction of the Harper-Johnson family tree. In both instances, Harper's "Psalm" speaks to Ostriker's understanding of the Psalms. The poet's sense of psalms as an expressive mode that is, at once, changing and constant becomes evident through the course of his poem:

> Strange
> that a harp
> of a thousand strings
> should stay
> in tune
> so long. (119)

Harper's "Psalm" demonstrates the poet's interest in questions of endurance and change over time. The poem gestures to a transcendent sense of tradition and kinship that informs the poet's body of work. Whether these connections emerge from branches on the poet's family tree or through kinships rooted in Black expression, Harper's poetry works to acknowledge these oscillations between poetic possibility and demonstratable conditions.

Given the publication context of *I Do Believe in People,* "Psalm" finds an intimate alignment with the poet's parents, especially his mother, whose Bible held the family's figurations of lineage, recording couplings, births, and deaths. The poem speaks equivocally to questions the poet raises about tradition and ancestry throughout his project. At the same time, understanding the poem's engagement with the blues-rooted impulses of his poetic project, "Psalm" also speaks to Harper's "subjective correlative" concept. The poem looks to "expand the dialogue" by exploring tradition, identity, and improvisation (122). As such, "Psalm" demonstrates the poet's willingness to embrace "risks" through the "subjective correlative." In the Treseler interview, Harper identifies Robert Hayden as another Black poet who also pursues this dynamic. Explaining that Hayden's verse maintains a "slant affinity to modernism as practiced by the ancestors," Harper suggests his body of work illustrates the "need to innovate, to improvise." He reminds Treseler that this approach to writing verse "takes tremendous courage, particularly if you have been studious as Hayden was in learning the craft" ("Office Hours," 122).

In addition to bringing his poetic project into conversation with Hayden's work through the "subjective correlative," Harper also regards their poetry as maintaining a shared interest in locating, preserving, and commemorating Black identities within American experience. Harper understands his poetic project as holding ties to Hayden's through their work with commemorative and occasional verse, especially the elegy. By giving voice to the psalmist as they do, these poems further amplify connections linking these poets and their work. Harper's sense of Hayden's archival and memorial poetry is confirmed by Daniel Boorstin. Speaking in October 1976 at an event celebrating Hayden, and his appointment as Consultant in Poetry at the Library of Congress, Boorstin addresses what he sees as the distinguishing characteristics of Hayden's verse. The twelve-term Librarian of Congress suggests: "Every age must decide the role of the poet for itself. Greeks used the word for a poet that was synonymous with the word for maker. We have not really developed our own word for the Poet. I would like to think that our poet is our remembrancer. . . . In our age we need a poet to remind us of our tie to the past, our tie to all other human be-ings, our tie to the poets of other ages" (Boorstin, "Introduction upon Robert Hayden's Appointment," 16).

Harper echoes Boorstin's thoughts in "Every Shut-Eye Ain't Asleep / Every Good-Bye Ain't Gone: Robert Hayden [1913–1980]," the introduction to the special issue of *Obsidian* that Harper edited and dedicated to the poet, who died in February 1980. The essay depicts Hayden as a "remembrancer" and "custodian of consciousness," celebrating his poetry's ability to locate and identify the significance of sites, spaces, people, and occasions that would have otherwise been unnoticed. Harper writes that Hayden "wanted to collect all the poems from his old neighborhood, Paradise Valley . . . into a special collection that he wanted to give to his friends." According to Harper, this gift of a col-lection was to include "not only 'Elegies for Paradise Valley' . . . but 'Free Fan-tasia: Tiger Flowers,' 'Homage to the Empress of the Blues' and 'The Rabbi'" (10). Focusing on Hayden's poetic impulse to capture and archive imagery and figures, Harper brings attention to the elder poet's "love for what he called 'the folk idiom'" and "the folk person."

Harper regards Hayden's verse as collecting and artfully inscribing Black experience upon American consciousness. He explains: "Hayden's adapted bal-lade [in the fifth elegy from 'Elegies for Paradise Valley'] gives voice to the no-bility of the lowborn; [his] ballades also extend the tradition to include sections of emphasis—a re-evaluation of the 'tragic mulatto' stereotype in 'The Ballad of Sue Ellen Westerfield,' or the gothic mysticism of the old testament vision-ary persona in 'The Ballad of Nat Turner'" (Harper, "Every Shut-Eye Ain't Asleep," 12). Harper considers the distinguished catalogue of figures found in Hayden's verse as undertaking a particular form of memory work. He suggests that these efforts—evident in poems such as "Frederick Douglass," "Homage to the Empress of the Blues," "El-Hajj Malik El-Shabazz (Malcolm X)" and his tour de force of the transatlantic slave trade, "Middle Passage"—illustrate

Hayden's literary engagement with both Black experience and American memory. Speaking to Hayden's poetic ambition to equitably integrate these figures into a representative discussion of American national identity, Harper ultimately links his own verse to the elder poet's body of work in their poetry's shared pursuit of emotional contingencies and spontaneous transitions, resembling those that Ostriker associates with the Psalms.

These links emerge from the extended poetic conversation that the two poets conduct through poems such as Harper's "In Hayden's Collage," "Healing Song," and "Memorial Meetings" as well as "Free Fantasia: Tiger Flowers," which Hayden wrote for Harper. This exchange has its roots in Harper's initial encounter with Hayden, which occurred after a poetry reading at the University of Michigan in 1971. In "Every Shut-Eye Ain't Asleep," Harper recounts this meeting, writing that he approached the elder poet following the reading's conclusion and introduced himself: "'Mr. Hayden, it's a great honor to meet you, to have you come to my reading. You are a great poet—would you sign WORDS IN MORNING TIME [sic] for me. [sic]' Taking his WORDS in hand and smiling [sic] he said 'I was prepared not to like you'" (9). This encounter between Harper and Hayden was the beginning of a sustained dialogue, which proved to be literary, professional, and personal.

Correspondence between the poets is preserved, in part, by Xavier Nicholas in "Robert Hayden and Michael S. Harper: A Literary Friendship." This collection includes letters that date from October 1972 through February 11, 1980, just two weeks before Hayden's death. It charts the two poets' relationship, illustrating the genuine affection and profound kinship that developed between them. These bonds are evident, for example, in the letter from Hayden to Harper, dated June 19, 1974, that includes the poem "Tiger Flowers." Responding to Hayden on July 4, 1974, Harper praises the elder poet, writing enthusiastically: "I love that poem, a difficult grinding, poignant statement. Thank God language is still created in this low time of rhetoric and inanity" (988). Harper ultimately replied in kind, sending literary dedications and poetic responses to Hayden many times over the course of his career. "Message to Robert Hayden," a poem from *Nightmare Begins Responsibility* (1975), stands as the first published installment of this exchange.

Opening Harper's channel of poetic communication with the elder poet, "Message to Robert Hayden" appears in the "Sterling Letters" section of the *Nightmare* volume. The poem incorporates the variable tones and equivocal emotions that Ostriker associates with the Psalms. These impulses become evident as Harper's speaker delivers his "message" to Hayden in the course of the poem's two eight-line stanzas. Blending styles and sentiments, "Message to

Robert Hayden" arrives as a poetic hybrid: part intimate correspondence, part elegy, lament, and praise poem. Written to mark the passing of the Harlem Renaissance | New Negro Movement figure Arna Bontemps, Harper's literary missive begins:

> Do I make connections
> only after Arna's death
> electric with thanks
> for his warning loud
> handclasp on the porch
> weight, waiting in Nashville
> words of power lines
> down, sparks invisible (91)

In the poem's opening stanza, Harper's speaker references the "power lines" that he regards as sustaining Black expressive tradition. The poet affirms that, despite Bontemps's death and the undeniable loss it brings, the fundamental "connections" he understands as informing Black literary networks remain unbroken.

Recalling that Bontemps passed away in 1973, as Harper was gaining increased prominence as a Black poet and figure within American letters, the poem maps intergenerational connections among Black writers. The "warning loud / handclasp" that the poet receives from Bontemps "on the porch/ . . . in Nashville" becomes a rite of passage, conferred on him by this celebrated contributor to the New Negro Movement and Harlem Renaissance. "Message to Hayden" delivers an account of kinship and history in which Harper's speaker serves as a witness to and participant in the making of Black letters. Despite being "electric with thanks" following his encounter with Bontemps, the elder poet's passing creates a void for Harper's speaker. With Bontemps's death— "a power line/ down"—the urgent charge of the poet's "message for Hayden" diminishes, becoming "sparks invisible."

As this sense of loss and breakage envelop both poem and poet, "Message to Robert Hayden" functions as a conduit of communication between and among Black poets. Bontemps's message is passed on—at least in part—as the poem's first stanza closes with an unpunctuated question. In the second stanza, the message continues raising questions while moving forward. Its ambiguities become apparent as the poem's speaker presents his Hayden figure—perhaps grief stricken—"lying, locked in your car," awaiting the arrival of his wife, Erma, to make a "keyed night visit." The image is at once cryptic and disturbing. Recalling, however, that Hayden's legendarily poor eyesight prevented him from holding a driver's license gives it a measure of context. The poem moves toward its conclusion:

> And now, thanks,
> the only death that makes
> this message riddling
> praise of musing
> over wires, down, always down:
> and we bury that spark to light, always to light. (91)

With the poem's final six lines, Bontemps's "message" continues to move in "riddling" fashion, through Harper to Hayden. It arrives with gratitude as the poet extends his "thanks" to Hayden along with "praise of musing/ over wires, down, always down." These three poets—distanced as they are by generation and geography—acknowledge their connections as they "bury" what the speaker describes as "the only death that makes / this message." This burial—referencing Bontemps's passing—does not extinguish "that spark," shared by the three poets as both Black men and Black artists.

These transcendent movements—"to light, always to light"—serve and become the poem's message of resilience and resistance as these sixteen lines turn and double back upon themselves. Referencing its points of diversion and connections, "Message to Robert Hayden" delivers a commentary on the circuitous mode of communications linking the poet to his literary kinsmen. While imbued with the profound sense of loss, "Message to Robert Hayden" gestures toward a sense of hope and endurance, which the poet locates in his investigation of the "invisible" networks of expression connecting Harper's speaker to Hayden and Bontemps.

Continuing to expand the scope of this project, Harper maps pathways traveled by expressive power in "Double Elegy." In the course of this poem from *Healing Song for the Inner Ear,* Harper's speaker again surveys contradictory and complementary lines of celebration and mourning. "Double Elegy" delivers an equivocal, psalmlike account of the lives and poetry of Robert Hayden and James Wright. As he does in "Message to Hayden," Harper's speaker simultaneously celebrates as he laments. However, having cultivated a distinct personal and professional relationship with each poet, Harper grieves their deaths more poignantly than he does that of Bontemps. "Double Elegy" becomes a means for the poet to reflect on Hayden and Wright, who passed away within weeks of one another during the winter of 1980.

In the poem's first stanza, Harper considers ways in which the two departed poets were alike, despite their profoundly different backgrounds, experiences, and identities:

> Whatever city or country road
> you two are on
> there are nettles,
> and the dark invisible
> elements cling to your skin
> though you do not cry
> and you do not scratch
> your arms at forty-five degree angles
> as the landing point of a swan
> in the Ohio, the Detroit River (14)

The poet situates both Hayden and Wright within the distinct environments from which they emerged. Wright walks along a "country road" beside the Ohio River, presumably near his hometown of Martinsville, Ohio; Hayden passes through his "city"—Detroit—and its river.

At the same time, Harper's speaker suggests that despite the strong ties connecting these poets to their homespaces, Hayden and Wright are not entirely at ease. Stoically enduring "nettles" and "dark invisible / elements clinging to [their] skin," both poets enter the poem as captives of circumstance. Confronting these irritants and hazards, the poets "do not cry," they "do not scratch." Instead, Harper's speaker acknowledges that, even in death—with their "arms at forty-five degree angles," assuming a pose that he likens to "the landing point of a swan"—Hayden and Wright both demonstrate their grace.

The second stanza of "Double Elegy" focuses on Hayden, referencing specific sites and figures from his life and poetry, such as the Paradise Theatre, an early- and mid-twentieth century Black music performance venue located in the Paradise Valley neighborhood of Detroit, where Hayden grew up. Similarly, Harper's speaker also evokes the Uncle Henry figure and his séance table, which appear in Hayden's poetic remembrance of his Detroit upbringing, "Elegy for Paradise Valley." Similarly, in the poem's third stanza, Harper's speaker recollects cutting capers with Wright in Minneapolis on a "subzero platform" and "at the Radisson Hotel." These postmortem reviews of the speaker's relationships with these poets allow Hayden and Wright to emerge from Harper's poem as multidimensional figures. In the fourth stanza of "Double Elegy," the depth and complexity of these poets and their projects becomes evident where Harper's speaker identifies points of common connection between Hayden and Wright:

> You two men like to confront
> the craters of history and spillage,

> our natural infections of you
> inoculating blankets and fur
> ethos of cadaver and sunflower. (15)

In these lines, the poet effectively performs "custodial duties" on behalf of the deceased poets, arising from the relationships that he cultivated with Hayden and Wright during the 1970s. In his essay, "Elective Kinship: Improvisations on History and Portraiture," Jonathan Blunk speaks to the sense of responsibility that Harper felt to uphold the two poets' memories and literary legacies.

Blunk's study examines connections between the three poets, suggesting that Hayden and Wright served as "companion spirits" for Harper. In "Elective Kinship," Blunk identifies their work as being informed by a kinship mode that mitigates the various categorical differences—racial, geographic, generational, and so on—that distinguished the poets from one another. For example, "Elective Kinship" examines the poverty that both Hayden and Wright knew as children in the early part of the twentieth century, recognizing it as a major point of intersection, linking both the poets and their projects. Accounting for the particular spiritual and aesthetic connections that these poets experienced to one another and in their work, Blunk quotes Harper as saying that both Hayden and Wright "shared a great respect for the working class, for everyday workers" (6). Blunk also points out that all three poets created indelible poetic portraits of their immediate families, specifically citing Hayden's "Those Winter Sundays" as well as Wright's "Youth," "Honey," and "Two Postures beside a Fire." According to Blunk, these poems ultimately intersect with Harper's project by revealing "the urgency both poets felt to tell the stories that need telling, about the people they knew and the hardships of their lives" (6).

"Elective Kinship" speaks to the poet's sense of connection to Hayden and Wright, expressed in the fifth and final stanza of "Double Elegy." Throughout this portion of the poem, Harper's speaker alters his mode of address, shifting away from the reserved, reflective, third-person accounts of the elder poets that appear earlier in the poem. Instead, exhibiting the profound sense of grief that he experiences following the deaths of Wright and Hayden, the poet demonstrates greater emotional engagement with his subject matter by using the first-person singular:

> I hold the dogwood blossom,
> eat the pear, and watch the nettle
> swim up in the pools of the completed song
> of Leadbelly and Little Crow (15)

Grappling with his sense of loss in these lines, the poet reaches toward his departed "companion spirits." With Wright and Hayden now passed, Harper's speaker turns to their verse. He witnesses their consolidation as "completed songs" sung by figures he associates with the poets' work. Hayden's understanding of blues-rooted expression summonses legendary Black music figure Huddie Leadbetter—better known as "Lead Belly"—into the poem. Similarly, considering Wright's sense of the inherent complexities of American experience, the poet conjures the figure of Little Crow or Taoyateduta (Mdewakanton Dakota), whose participation in the 1862 Dakota War against the US Army in Minnesota is memorialized in Wright's poem "A Centenary Ode."

Moving through these channels, Harper brings "Double Elegy" to its conclusion, evoking Hayden and Wright as Little Crow arrives "crooning" to "buffalo and horse" and Lead Belly performs "the melody of Irene." Their songs converge in a landscape where Harper's speaker locates the two poets and states "this is really goodbye." Having reached this conclusion, he delivers a five-line summation of the lives and work of his poetic kinsmen:

> I can see the precious stones
> of embolism and consumption
> the platinum wires of the mouth:
> in the flowing rivers, in the public baths
> of Ohio and Michigan. (15)

Listing their respective causes of death, "embolism and consumption," Harper's speaker begins uncoupling Hayden and Wright. He locates these poets' respective burial sites and the "precious stones" that mark them. "Double Elegy" concludes with the poet referencing Wright's celebrated volume *Shall We Gather at the River* and its treatment of trans-Appalachian life in the rural Ohio Valley, by stating that he "can see" Wright and "the flowing rivers" of southeastern Ohio. Harper's speaker similarly "sees" Hayden in "the public baths" of Detroit, concretizing the late poet's connection to the city's urban landscape, confirming his understanding of Hayden's sexual identity.[1] In the final line of "Double Elegy," Harper's speaker renders a double-edged, psalm-like combination of celebration and lament for the two poets. Affirming the points of convergence and disjuncture, simultaneously distinguishing and connecting the poets to and from one another, Harper's speaker writes them into their respective home states "of Ohio and Michigan."

In "Elective Kinship," Jonathan Blunk suggests that "Double Elegy" illustrates Harper's affinity for Wright and Hayden. Identifying sensibilities shared among the three poets, Blunk posits that they all saw themselves as "interlopers, outsiders and systematic makers" on the American literary land-scape (5). Reading "Double Elegy" with this in mind, the poem can be seen as commemorating the literary friendship of Wright, Hayden, and Harper. Blunk recognizes the poem as underscoring Harper's vision of literature as a vehicle capable of bridging multiple identity categories. "Double Elegy" speaks to the sustained engagement that Harper's verse exhibits with respect to generative kinship, across generational, racial, or geographic differences.

Given its content and sentiment, "Double Elegy" may be understood as a singular work within Michael S. Harper's poetic *oeuvre*. However, the poem's simultaneous expressions of celebration and mourning for Wright and Hayden are not entirely unique within his body of work. Harper consistently demon-strates this impulse to celebrate and grieve figures whom he identifies as kin, from *Dear John, Dear Coltrane* through *Use Trouble*. In these psalmlike, poetic portraits, the poet delivers accounts of the lives and work of writers and poets, visual artists, and musicians. Harper collects and considers the experiences of cultural practitioners representing a wide range of experiences, which includes "unheralded" artists—poet Ralph Dickey, for instance—as well as those whose work is "underappreciated"—novelist Leon Forrest is one example—along with "heralded figures " such as writers Philip Levine, Gwendolyn Brooks, and Richard Wright or collagist Romare Bearden.

With poems such as "Songline from a Tessera Journal," the "Heartblows" sequence, and "*mahalia:* MAHALIA," Harper registers the imprint that his "kin" leave on both his work and the project of constructing a more inclusive and representative American cultural landscape. Channeling generative kinship in this way, the poet creates and identifies features within and upon this terrain. Engaging expressive tradition, audiences, and cultural practitioners, Harper's verse examines dynamic interactions that connect these figures while com-memorating both works of art as well as the work of artists. "Use Trouble," the title poem from the last volume of verse Harper published in his lifetime, which opens with the epigraph "*for Jacob Armstead Lawrence / 1917–2000, in memoriam*" and explores the life and legacy of visual artist Jacob Lawrence in fourteen unrhymed couplets. An elegy, it delivers an account of Lawrence's artwork in a cascade of brief, staccato phrases:

> You told this to the children
> when they confessed their works
> were incomplete   your dignity   grace
> a mapped space   for trouble . . . (34)

Creating a seemingly incongruous trinity of "grace," "dignity," and "trouble," the poet locates these elements within Lawrence's body of work, including his teaching. "Use Trouble" makes a case that good art is "troublesome" and good artists are "trouble makers."

To support these claims, the poet examines the painter's epic, sixty-panel series of narrative images, entitled "The Migration of the Negro." In this painterly account of the Great Migration, Lawrence captures the impact that this movement from the rural South to the urban North had on Black people's lives and the shape of Black America. The "Migration" series serves as a backdrop for Harper's poem, ultimately allowing its speaker to bring Lawrence's life and work into conversation with those of Robert Hayden. In "Use Trouble" Hayden and Lawrence come to experience, express, and embody the list of racist contradictions, regional presumptions, and radical juxtapositions Black migrants from the rural South experienced as they arrived in northern cities.

Throughout Harper's poem, the poet and the painter—who both came of age in Black urban environments, after relocating to the North—serve as eye-witnesses to the migration process. At the same time "Use Trouble" also depicts these two Black artists' first-hand experience with the de facto segregation of northern cities. Hayden and Lawrence emerge from the poem as Black men in the United States who regularly encounter systemic obstacles that limit their exercise of citizenship rights and marginalize their expressive freedom. "Use Trouble" makes their artwork, at once, both troublesome and necessary.

> your *migration* series   at   23
> synaptic code for having nothing
> as you built off the backs of the poor
> your symmetries where paint was talk
> "gumbo yaya" Hayden (your collaborator)
> coined it about his native paradise valley . . . (34)

The poem's speaker addresses the cultural transformations that Hayden and Lawrence witnessed by living through the migration and the New Negro Movement. Locating their connections to working class Black enclaves, the poem presents poet and painter as receiving "nourishment" from "the Detroit ghetto" and "Harlem," respectively. Tracing Hayden and Lawrence's artistic development in terms of geography, generative kinship, and convergent history, the poem also references their collaboration on a limited-edition art book examining John Brown's 1859 raid on Harpers Ferry. The volume included Hayden's poem "John Brown" and twenty-two screen prints by Lawrence, depicting moments in the abolitionist's life.

"Use Trouble" exhibits the equivocal, psalmlike structure of Harper's other kinship-praise poems. The poet pursues this course, simultaneously celebrating Lawrence's life and work while lamenting his demise. He retraces Lawrence's

steps from Harlem to midtown Manhattan, recalling the "sixty-block walk to
MoMA" that the painter made as a youth in order to study at the Museum of
Modern Art (35). Presented in this way, the artist's movements to and from the
museum become a personal migration path toward his expressive vision. However, as triumphant as the details of Lawrence's rise may be, Harper's speaker
does not linger on the artist's past. Addressing the sad fact of Lawrence's passing, he states:

> now in Seattle they lay you down
> those parts Indian of your heritage
> in Chief Seattle's words:
> "This we know—
> All things are connected
> like the blood" (35)

Turning away from Lawrence's early life in New York and bringing attention
to his many years in Seattle, Harper's speaker focuses on the deep connections
that the painter developed to his adopted city.[2] These lines also gesture toward
the painter's vision of a multiracial, multiethnic American identity, which Lawrence explores in his art. Acknowledging these impulses expressed through the
painters work, the poet references Lawrence's Indigenous heritage and draws a
quote from Chief Seattle, namesake of Lawrence's adoptive city.

In the final four couplets of "Use Trouble," the poet delivers an overview of
Lawrence's career, assembling a collection of images that reference moments
and motifs from Lawrence's body of work. These moments converge as the
poem concludes:

> migraines at gunpoint
> bullet-ridden   love song   as migrants
> to the highest plane
> a vast battlefield of tones
> vegetation of the visible where
> there is no insurance
> yet   in retrospective   fantasy
> to remake the spirit in your name (35)

Conveying his sense that the artist and his work reach "the highest plane,"
Harper's speaker reflects on the connections he maintains with the painter's
biographical and thematic studies of Black experience. He references several of
Lawrence's most important works, including his *Toussaint L'Ouverture* series
(1937–38) and *The Harriet Tubman* series (1939–40), along with his master
work, *The Migration of the Negro* (1940–41) and the lesser known *War* series

(1946–47). The final couplet of the poem arrives, fully loaded, and Harper delivers his evaluation of Lawrence's work as "troubling" received notions about Black life and American experience.

By extension, "Use Trouble" curates a poetic "retrospective" for Lawrence and his work, linking the artist to the spirit of his biblical namesake, Jacob. Harper's speaker makes a comparison between the bold and determined actions of these two Jacobs. Both Jacob, patriarch of the Israelites, and Jacob Lawrence, the artist, may be understood as "troublemakers." With Lawrence working to "remake the spirit in [his] name," Harper completes his tribute to the Black visual artist, effectively adding his name to his list of kinsmen. At the same time, Harper's speaker also acknowledges that struggle—and trouble—are necessary to the process of producing transformational cultural works.

Donna Seaman's review of *Use Trouble* identifies the complex "both/and" impulse that informs the title piece of Harper's final volume of verse. Locating this movement throughout the collection, Seaman writes: "Whether he is telling nuanced tales of friends or family or celebrating the awakening power of art, Harper perceives life's interconnectivity of sorrow and joy" (22). These dueling sentiments are also evident in "Sherley Anne Williams: 1944–1999," another elegy, like "Use Trouble," in the volume's second section. In this poem, the poet once again mourns and celebrates the life and work of a recently departed Black artist. Through the fourteen short, unrhymed couplets comprising "Sherley Anne Williams," Harper's speaker commemorates this novelist, poet, and critic. Once again striking the equivocal tones of the psalm, the poet opens the work with an account of Williams's upbringing, in and around the cotton fields of Kern County, California:

> Worshipped |in the fields
> sometimes |in darkness
> heat |at highnoon
> killing fields |but after water
> florescent |crops
> braceros |picked. . . (68)

Focusing on Williams's first-hand knowledge of living conditions in the cotton producing portions of California's Central Valley, the poet reflects on her youth. Harper's speaker recalls verse Williams published in volumes such as *The Peacock Poems* and *Some One Sweet Angel Chile* as well as her Caldecott prize-winning, illustrated children's book *Working Cotton.*

Through these works and others, Williams brings attention to twentieth-century cotton production in the United States, marking and mapping the life ways of farm workers and their children. Harper's poem acknowledges

Williams's movements on pathways traveled by "braceros" and the other agricultural workers she knew during her formative years. In this way, the poet
recognizes Williams's literary project as reframing prevailing images of mid-
twentieth-century California life. Her portraits of Black and Latinix farm
workers tending cotton plants pose a counternarrative to popular notions of
the Golden State's endless summers and surf safaris. Harper's speaker sees
these mythic images wilting in the "heat/ at highnoon."

In "Sherley Anne Williams," Harper presents an expansive collection of
personal memories that sustain his relationship with the late poet. He expresses
his admiration for Williams and her work:

> put you in every book
> I could read or write
> remember
> commentaries
> at public tables
> in and out of the University (68)

Harper links her memory to the many Black artists his other psalmlike elegies
commemorate. The poet's high regard for Williams, expressed in the assertion
that he "put [her] in every book /[he] could read or write," becomes further un-
derscored by considering the place that the poem occupies within *Use Trouble*.
It is placed in the volume's second section, among poems dedicated to Toni
Morrison ("Chloe: Black Pastoral Luminous," and "Handmade Book on the
Theme of the Beloved"), Ralph Ellison ("Archives: Public Library I" and "Archives: Public Library II"), and Jay Saunders Redding ("Portrait: (Jay Saunders
Redding Sayles Hall) 5/26/97," "Esther," "Triumphs," and "Homage to Jay
Saunders Redding on His Natal Day: 10 13 04"). Harper's elegy for Williams
stands with poems composed for these and other well-known Black writers.

In the poem's final couplets, the poet continues to express his admiration
for Williams:

> outtakes are best
> your heart a map
> ancestors
> weeping (69)

These lines demonstrate Harper's poetic capacity for remembrance. "Sherley
Anne Williams" offers a reflection of the late poet's under-discussed contributions to Black letters. The poem expresses the sense of both collective
and individual loss that ensues from her passing. Harper's speaker identifies
Black music ("outtakes are best"), geography and landscape ("your heart a

map"), and Black expressive tradition ("ancestors / weeping") emerging from Williams's varied body of work. These insights gain an additional measure of context by recalling that Harper, along with Sterling A. Brown, served on Williams's Master of Arts thesis committee at Brown University. Williams would go on to publish a revised version of the thesis she prepared under Harper and Brown's direction as *Give Birth to Brightness: A Thematic Study in Neo-Black Literature.*

Reading poetry, fiction, and drama by James Baldwin, Amiri Baraka, and Ernest J. Gaines, *Give Birth to Brightness* addresses a set of connections that Williams identifies within Black cultural production as a whole and Black literature in particular. Writing in the early 1970s, at a moment of intense debate about Black expression, Williams was keenly aware of the tensions invested in generational and factional conversations taking place between and among Black writers, musicians, and artists. In the introduction to her study, Williams acknowledged the strong responses—both pro and con—that creative and critical work aligned with the Black Arts Movement received and explained that in *Give Birth to Brightness,* "emphasis is placed on continuity." The study discusses what she calls "Neo-Black literature," which she defines as "the continuous tradition of Black literature—both fiction and non-fiction, prose and poetry" (22).

Similarly, in the "Author's Afterword," Williams speaks directly to this sense of continuity. Appealing for Black critics to recognize points of common understanding rather than particular differences during a high moment of Black Arts Movement–era discord, she asserts: "Our most important function . . . lies in examining the works of [Black] writers to see how well they present their versions of Black life . . . It is these inner views of ourselves, which we must now address" (238–39). Williams also connects her study to the legacy of Sterling A. Brown and the expansive, integrative perspectives on literature, criticism, and culture that inform in his poetry, scholarship, and folkloric work. This impulse is evident on the volume's dedication page, where she writes: "In another time and some other place, this book would have been dedicated to Professor Sterling Brown, whose quiet questioning and prodding during interminable summer days forced me to clarify, expand and define" (7). Williams thanks Brown—along with Nathan Heard and Leah King—for facilitating the completion of her book project. She explains that her study would have been "very difficult to create" without their input. She dedicates the volume to her son, Malcolm.

Exploring "Neo-Black literature" and building upon the elder poet's foundational examinations of Black music and Black folklife, Williams's study establishes connections to Brown's legacy. At the same time, her project expands upon his work in critical pieces such as "Negro Folk Expression" and "Stray Notes on Jazz" while amplifying Brown's poetic explorations of the blues from *Southern Road*. In her volume's afterword Williams encapsulates her sense of the blues and its relationship to Black expressive culture: "I swear that Baraka's poem, "leroy," tells me the same thing as Richard's speech in the third act of [Baldwin's] *Blues for Mr. Charlie* . . . both touch the same theme as Lightnin' Hopkins version of "Going Down Slow" (237). Recognizing the blues as a mode, Williams's study traces this common thread across genres and generations.

In this way, the blues shape *Give Birth to Brightness,* aligning Williams's project with Brown's body of work. By extension—through the poems he's dedicated to Brown and his exploration of blues-rooted expression—these links bind Williams and Harper. This interlocking set of cross references and poetic gestures effectively illustrate the dynamism of the kinship mode. With Williams, like Harper, claiming Brown as her literary kinsman, Harper's efforts to honor Brown ties his work to Williams and her endeavors to promote "continuity" among Black writers and Black literary projects.

These connections are enhanced by recalling that in the 1970s and '80s Harper was instrumental in generating the renewed interest in Brown's poetry and criticism that lasted into the twenty-first century. Harper's editorial work on *The Collected Poems of Sterling A. Brown,* published by the National Poetry Series, helped spark this attention. The volume not only returned Brown's verse to circulation, it also initiated conversations about work from his late New Negro era volume, *A Southern Road,* and *The Last Ride of Wild Bill,* a collection published by Broadside Press during the Black Arts Movement. At the same time, *The Collected Poems* also brought *No Hiding Place* into print for the first time.[3]

Harper's "Integer Is a Whole Number" provides insight into the poet's efforts to edit *The Collected Poems* with Brown. In this essay from John Edgar Tidwell and Steven Tracy's collection *After Winter: The Art and Life of Sterling A. Brown,* Harper relates the sense of dread that filled Brown before the volume went to press. He writes: "Sterling and I built his manuscript—from three handwritten notebooks—on an Olivetti typewriter that I had brought in baggage on a commuter flight from Providence to National Airport. Sterling would constantly delay, debating whether to include [one poem or another] . . . Sterling had a sense that his *Collected Poems* would never see the light of day. Even after I had selected his book, the project had no publisher" (279). Working closely in this improvisational fashion, Harper and Brown established their close connections.

Robert Stepto addresses the personal and literary ties shared by the two poets in "Michael Harper's Extended Tree: John Coltrane and Sterling Brown," bringing attention to "Br'er Sterling and the Rocker." As the first poem in the "Sterling Letters" section of *Nightmare Begins Responsibility*, "Br'er Sterling and the Rocker" presents the elder poet with a double-edged invitation to re-enter the dialogue on Black literature and culture, after his extended hiatus. The poem also testifies to the support that Brown received from his spouse, Daisy. This process begins in the poem's dedication, which reads "for Sterling A. and Daisy T. Brown / 16 June 1973."

Throughout the poem, Harper's speaker acknowledges Brown's mastery of the ballad, understanding of Black folk culture, and knowledge of the blues. Harper's speaker simultaneously encourages Brown to return to work, while imploring him to tend to his literary legacy. Bringing attention to the "boomerang-like" movement of history and culture, Harper's speaker focuses on Brown's rocking chair. He depicts it as a hybrid boomerang that both marks the elder poet's inactivity and holds the key to his return to the literary world:

> Any fool knows a Br'er in a rocker
> is a boomerang incarnate;
> look at the blade of the rocker,

The poem begins delivering its variation on the "history as boomerang" motif that Ralph Ellison outlines in the prologue of *Invisible Man*.[4] Assessing the condition of "Br'er Sterling," Harper extends his double-edged, psalmlike message to the elder poet.

Simultaneously imploring and encouraging "Br'er Sterling" to take action, the poem effectively documents Brown's first steps toward re-entering conversations concerning American poetry and Black culture. "Br'er Sterling and the Rocker," which the poet understood as a "folk sonnet,"[5] chronicles Brown's movements away from his rocker and out of "retirement." The poem accounts for Harper's efforts to return the elder poet's attention to literary endeavors. This impulse becomes evident in these lines:

> To speak of poetry is the curled line straightened,
> to speak of double talk, the tongue pure,
> gone pure, the stoic line a trestle
> whistlin', a man a train comin' on: (79)

Reminding the Brown figure of the rarified place he and his work hold within Black Letters, Harper's speaker seeks to bridge the gap separating Brown from the literary world. The depth of alienation that Brown felt sitting in his "rocker" becomes evident; he recalls that when the elder poet met Harper at the 1972 Black Academy of Arts and Letters awards ceremony in New York, he introduced himself as the "Invisible Mr. Brown."

The poet continues his double-edged celebration and exhortation efforts in the closing stanzas of "Br'er Sterling and the Rocker." He acknowledges the critical role that Brown's spouse, "Miss Daisy," holds within these efforts to dislodge the elder poet from his self-imposed isolation:

> Listen Br'er Sterling
> steel-drivin' man, folk-said, folk-sayin',
> that chair's a blues-harnessed star
> turnin' on its earthly axis;
> Miss Daisy, latch on that star's arc,
> hold on sweet mama; Br'er Sterling's rocker glows. (79)

Devoting their energy and attention to both Sterling Brown the man and Sterling Brown the literary figure, Harper and "Miss Daisy" successfully revived interest in Brown's work as a critic, poet, teacher, and scholar. Their efforts facilitated the "come back" that Harper's speaker presents to Brown in "Br'er Sterling and the Rocker."

Harper continued to work closely with Brown until his death in January 1989. The poet recorded various phases of Sterling Brown's personal renaissance with other poems from the "Sterling Letters" section of *Nightmare Begins Responsibility*, such as "BROWN at Brown" and "WILLIAMS COLLEGE: after 51 years—." Speaking with Charles Rowell during their 1991 *Callaloo* interview, Harper was asked to reflect on his relationship with Brown. Recalling a visit to the poet's home in Washington, DC that he made during the early 1970s along with novelist Ernest J. Gaines, Harper informs Rowell that when he asked Brown "to read and lecture" at Brown University, the elder poet initially declined because, according to Harper, "Sterling said he wasn't a poet anymore" (Rowell, "'Down Don't Worry Me'," 797). However, after Harper assured him that he and his work would be welcomed, Brown traveled to Providence and engaged an audience away from the Howard University campus and his familiar rocking chair. As a result, "Br'er Sterling" began reclaiming his position as a resource and presence within conversations about Black poetry, Black expression, and the New Negro Movement.

Brown's reentry into these dialogues renewed interest in his work, prompting reevaluations of his career as a critic, poet, teacher, and scholar. As Brown's poetry returned to print, a sustained examination and appreciation of his literary legacy followed, beginning with the publication of Joanne V.

Gabbin's *Sterling A. Brown: Building the Black Aesthetic Tradition*. The wave of scholarly interest in Brown's work that followed Gabbin's study included Mark A. Sanders, *A Son's Return: Selected Essays of Sterling A. Brown* and a special volume of *Callaloo* dedicated to Brown's poetic and scholarly legacy. Where Sanders's edited collection focused on critical and scholarly work Brown published in *Phylon* and *Opportunity* at mid-century, the *Callaloo* number featured commemorative poetry by Harper and Sonia Sanchez, two interviews with Brown—one with Rowell and one with John Edgar Tidwell—in addition to essays on Brown's work by Robert Stepto, Kimberly W. Benston, John Callahan, and others. It also included talks from a symposium on Brown's life and work with contributions from a list of prominent scholars and critics, including Eleanor Holmes Norton, Paula Giddings, Sterling Stuckey, Wahneema Lubiano, and Cornel West. Shortly after the *Callaloo* special came into print, Sanders's monograph, *Afro-Modernist Aesthetics and the Poetry of Sterling A. Brown,* was published. Sanders and Tidwell coedited Brown's unpublished Jim Crow–era travelogues as *Sterling A. Brown's A Negro Looks at the South*. Tidwell then teamed up with Steven C. Tracy to coedit their critical compendium, *After Winter: The Art and Life of Sterling A. Brown*.

As these publications appeared, Harper continued to champion efforts to improve and expand understandings of Brown's work and legacy. Five years after Brown's death, Harper published *Honorable Amendments,* which includes a psalmlike elegy written in honor of the departed poet, entitled "To an Old Man Twiddlin' Thumbs." The poem bears witness to the multilayered kinship bonds connecting the two poets. Like "Br'er Sterling and the Rocker," the poem underscores the links Harper and Brown maintained with one another by incorporating members of their respective families into the poem. "Twiddlin' Thumbs" captures a sense of Harper's engagement with the elder poet while at the same time conveying a sense of Brown's estrangement from the literary world, which kept him "in his rocker."

Reiterating the sense of isolation that Brown felt into his later life, "Twiddlin' Thumbs" speaks to the alternating sense of tension and tedium that came to define the elder poet's experience of the world around him. These conditions become evident in the poem's opening stanza:

> You sit twiddlin' thumbs
> "beat out," watching
> your wife, watch you watch her:
> all this watching twiddlin' thumbs. (25)

Unlike "Br'er Sterling and the Rocker," Brown is not explicitly named as the subject of this poem. Instead, its "Brown-like figure" remains unnamed throughout the course of "Twiddlin' Thumbs." Yet despite its ultra-thin veil of anonymity, the poem's opening stanza allows the poet to underscore his connections with the Brown-like figure in ways that bring "Twiddlin' Thumbs" into conversation with "Br'er Sterling and the Rocker."

Connections between both the two poems and the two poets expand and intensify as Harper incorporates family members, both his own and those of the Brown-like figure, into these works. In "Br'er Sterling and the Rocker," the two poets relationship becomes enhanced by the poet's references to Brown's spouse, "Miss Daisy." Similarly, in "Twiddlin' Thumbs" Miss Daisy is present along with Harper's children, sons Roland and Patrice, and his daughter, Rachel. Brown's wife and Harper's children illustrate the two poets' level of comfort with each other. They witness the Brown-like figure's capacity to act out his boredom and isolation through obstinance. The elder poet's fragility becomes fully evident:

> My children fidget while you balance
> thumb controls on local news,
> excerpts from a recent book on slavery,
> and we finally have scale of twiddlin' thumbs. (25)

Accessing a "scale of twiddlin' thumbs" in this way, the poem delivers an intergenerational perspective on a Brown-like figure, who makes "children fidget" by directing gestures and glances toward his wife as "a recent book on slavery" is discussed on television. Recalling that Brown's father—Sterling N. Brown—was enslaved upon his birth in eastern Tennessee establishes a context for "all this watching." The introduction to the *Collected Poems* provides a bit more background: historian Sterling Stuckey explains that the elder Brown, "unlike many of similar origin, was not ashamed of his slave heritage nor was he ashamed of rural Negro descendants of slaves" (Harper 9).

In the third stanza of "Twiddlin' Thumbs," Harper's speaker addresses the Brown-like figure in a manner reminiscent of, but not entirely similar to, "Br'er Sterling and the Rocker." While the poet admonishes and implores his Brown-like figure in both poems, throughout "Twiddlin' Thumbs" the elder poet receives unvarnished advice from Harper concerning the psycho-chemical dimensions of his condition. The second poem, presents the elder poet's emotional well-being in greater detail:

> Old man, remember the chemistry
> for your depression is alchemical.
> I set out my convivial tools
> measuring your need, measuring your index (25)

The Brown-like figure in "Twiddlin' Thumbs" emerges with greater definition than the elder poet depicted in "Br'er Sterling and the Rocker." Referencing a diagnosis of clinical depression and an account of the awkward, tense exchanges between the elder poet, Harper, and their family members, the psychological condition of the Brown figure becomes evident.

Recalling that "Twiddlin' Thumbs" was published after Brown's death helps to account for this shift in perspective. The poem speaks to intimate connections that existed between Brown and Harper. The elder poet's sense of "invisibility" becomes more tangible while the speaker's efforts to (re)animate the Brown figure's interest in literary conversation using "convivial tools" gains context. As the third stanza continues, Harper goes on to account for the support that the elder poet received from his wife. Taking note of her "slavery of affection," the poet delivers a more detailed portrait of "Miss Daisy." This sketch receives additional context from Harper's "An Integer Is a Whole Number," in which Brown's volatility and Miss Daisy's sensitivity are recalled; she "translated his mood in milliseconds" (275).

In the fourth and final stanza of "Twiddlin' Thumbs," Harper delivers his unvarnished analysis of the Brown-like figure, acknowledging his clinical depression:

> Old Man, my pestle works for your recovery;
> old man, the conjure knowledge is
> "beat out" with alkaline and tea,
> this nightmare where you've lost your way home:
> old man, the strong men must come on. (25)

Once again, the poem presents the Brown figure as needing support. The severity of his situation becomes evident as Harper "works" for the elder poet's "recovery." Effectively serving as a hybrid shaman | literary-pharmacist, prescribing a combination of folk wisdom ("conjure knowledge") and chemical tinctures ("alkaline and tea"), he seeks to release the elder poet from the "nightmare" of his depression. In its attempt to refresh and awaken the elder poet, the poem concludes with Harper deliberately delivering a riff on Brown's poem "Strong Men," reminding the "old man" that "the strong men must come on."

In this way, the "both/and" sensibility that the poet brings to his Brown-like figure in "Twiddlin' Thumbs" enters a conversation with the psalmlike qualities of elegies and praise poems he dedicates to Robert Hayden, James Wright, Jacob Lawrence, and Sherley Anne Williams. Addressing his kinspeople as he does in these poems, the poet contacts the "emotional turbulence" that Ostriker identifies as a critical component of the Psalms in her essay, "Psalm and Anti-Psalm." Working as a psalmist, Harper generates a particular set of "voicings," delivering "the joy and despair and hope and frustration and fear and anger and grief and sorrow" (11) that Ostriker associates with the Psalms. The poet also explores these modes of expression in the course of the poetic conversation that he conducts with Gwendolyn Brooks throughout his body of work.

Harper wrote and dedicated poems to Brooks over the course of his career, identifying the Pulitzer Prize-winning poet as his "champion." Harper presents various accounts—in both prose and verse—of Brooks ushering the manuscript that would become *Dear John, Dear Coltrane* from the slush pile of the 1970 United States Poetry Contest through the publication process at the University of Pittsburgh Press. While repeatedly expressing his gratitude for Brooks's unsolicited support, Harper acknowledges her impactful action in poems published during both the earlier and later stages of his career. These titles include "Madimba: Gwendolyn Brooks" from *History Is Your Own Heartbeat,* the "Sorbet sequence"—"Sorbet," "Double Sorbet," and "Triple Sorbet"—found in *Songlines in Michaeltree,* and three poems—"Wizardry: The Poetic Saga in Song of Gwendolyn Brooks," "The Poet's Voice" and "Zen: The *Trainride* Home to the Welcome Table"—that appear in *Use Trouble.*

Considered as a group, these works reflect the poet's evolving sense of Brooks and her body of work. For example, in "Madimba" and "*Trainride*"— the first and final poems that Harper published and dedicated to Brooks during his lifetime—the elder poet receives praise that arrives in language marking their kinship. Standing as the bookends of Harper's poetic commentary on Brooks's literary persona, these poems respectively present her as "*Double-conscious sister in the veil*" and "our holy ghost / champeen." However, in the three "Sorbet poems," Harper delivers a different take. In these more intimate and personalized sketches of Brooks, Harper's speaker brings attention to a set of specific engagements and exchanges between the two poets. As such, the "Sorbet sequence" examines Brooks through the generative kinship mode, presenting a set of shared sentiments and common experiences as the bonds of their relationship.

In "The Poet's Voice" Harper approaches Brooks's verse in yet another manner. This poem, found among new works in the "Peace Gene" section of *Songlines in Michaeltree,* recognizes the complex position that Brooks occupies within the American literary landscape by virtue of being both a Black woman and a poet. "The Poet's Voice" signals its distinct perspective on her poetic legacy by opening with an epigraph that reads "love, light, loss, liberty, lunacy / and laceration." Using these lines, which appeared in Brooks's contribution to a special forty-fifth anniversary volume of *Ebony* magazine, Harper's speaker brings a "both/and" sensibility to this exploration of the poet and her verse. He pursues this impulse in the poem's opening couplet: "Too much made of birth in Topeka / too little made of Chicago *Defender*" (263). In the eleven couplets that follow, Harper's speaker presents a summary of Brooks's body of work and career, identifying her uncanny capacity to be at once both "ahead" and "behind" with respect to particular literary trends or sensibilities.

In "The Poet's Voice," Harper renders his account of the various phases of Brooks career. He bears witness to the painstaking precision Brooks brought to her work—"clipping / microscopic tintypes of losses and gains"—and identifies her efforts as those of a visionary artist. He describes Brooks's verse as being "without the slightest naivete" and "of the street, backyard, parlor grid." Harper's speaker, then, enthusiastically asserts:

> her masterpiece of the "singing tree"
> "We Real Cool" in 1959 anticipates the rest of the century (263)

"The Poet's Voice" recognizes the personal and aesthetic transformations that Brooks undertook during the Black Arts Movement. Harper writes that "after Fisk in 1967"[6] Brooks was "known by detractors and sycophants / alike as 'Mother Afrika'" (263). Seeking to move beyond the almost stereotyped limitations of discussing Brooks's career "after Fisk" in through the lens of a "detractor/sycophant" binary, Harper's speaker continues, describing the poet's later life and work: "she remains a citizen in daily / interiors of unassailable synapse" (263).

Amplifying his praise for Brooks's poetry in "The Poet's Voice," Harper describes her work as "contralto arpeggios released / in bemused attributes of light / at the end of her Lincoln West Tunnel" (263). He proclaims Brooks to be a "wordsmith of the 'real thing' / exhortingly brave in every territory / for those unsung in service evermore." Identifying Brooks's poetry as delivering interpretations of convergent history and generative kinship, Harper presents her project as both a model and catalyst for the verse that he aspires to produce. Sharon Olds addresses Brooks's body of work in similar terms in her short essay "Notes on Gwendolyn Brooks." Writing in Quraysh Ali Lansana and Sandra Jackson-Opoku's collection, *Revise the Psalm: Work Celebrating the Writing of Gwendolyn Brooks,* Olds examines "the riches—sometimes the horrors—of the worlds in [Brooks's] poems" (262). Suggesting that "[Brooks's] poems give profound enlightenment and pleasure to her readers," Olds identifies a both/and dynamic—not unlike Harper's—as informing the poet's project. She asserts that in Brooks's verse, the poet's "intelligence is impeccable, her imagination sparkly, her ear true" (262).

Olds's essay engages the discussion of Brooks's poetry that Harper delivers in his five-stanza praise poem, "Wizardry: The Poetic Saga in Song of

Gwendolyn Brooks." In this poem from the "Peace Gene" section of *Songlines in Michaeltree,* Harper acknowledges Brooks as his benefactor and behind-the-scenes advocate, recognizing the efforts she undertook on his behalf as fundamentally altering the trajectory of his literary career. As such, in "Wizardry" presents Harper presents his project as an extension of Brooks's verse. In the poem, the elder poet's words are presented in capital letters; in this way, she offers instruction and guidance to Harper on procedure and process. Her words reverberate from the first line of the poem: "You were my clear winner," once again acknowledging Brooks's role in establishing the trajectory of Harper's career. At the same time, throughout "Wizardry" the poet also offers commentary on the nebulous realm of literary contests.

Addressing the politics of editorial mandates and aesthetic frameworks, the speaker captures echoes reverberating from the intervention that Brooks performed on his behalf after the results of the 1970 United States Poetry Contest were announced. He recalls "the special meaning / of your bold HOLD ON!" that Brooks passed on to Harper in the letter, which, ultimately, defined his career. The weight and power of Brooks's "wizardry" emerges from the poem:

> a telegram followed, wanting to publish,
> but I held out for the critical word
> from your typewriter. (261)

In the second and third stanzas of "Wizardry," the poet shifts away from this discussion of the formative events of his career, offering instead an account of Black America's interior geography. "Wizardry" moves swiftly, from Brooks's birthplace in Topeka, Kansas to a set of points in Mississippi that includes Tupelo, Natchez, and Hattiesburg. Harper identifies sites within these boundaries as being "in the mecca." Referencing Brooks's epic, poetic account of the Great Migration and Chicago's South Side, the poet works to expand the historical footprint of his poem.

Harper's speaker identifies a solemn, discrete, and yet entirely foundational set of connections linking his project to Brooks. He identifies space and time—"at vespers," "through the floorboards"—before conjuring sites where Black women "gave their children up." Working in this way, Harper's speaker effectively doubles down on and doubles back within Brooks's body of work. In addition to referencing Pepita's mother and her futile, frantic search for the murdered child that takes place through the course of "In the Mecca," the poet also gestures to Brooks's poem "The Mother." By doing so, "Wizardry" takes full measure of Brooks's significance as both the subject of this poem and as a literary figure in her own right.

Throughout the course of "Wizardry" Harper casts a spell that converges in his poem's fourth stanza. He recalls a visit to the "Brooklyn College campus" where he "spoke about the South African / connection with my ancestors." Establishing these boundaries, he prepares to take flight, soaring through those regions of Black America that Ellison describes as "the territory." Collecting and connecting its imagery to Brooks's body of poetic work, he states:

> the AME bishopry|
> had its gangster bishops|
> who sang their own religion,
> with or without the spirit|
> which rose to buzzard's
> roost, to the rafters,
> and on the choir's bench
> satin dolls, and rollaways
> of our deep song,
> louder than Bessie Smith's
> |"my house fell down and I can't live
> there no mo" (262)

Harper's varied assemblage of blues-rooted, jazz-inflected, sanctified imagery carries the reader to the poem's conclusion. Having established a sufficient level of tension through his listing and naming efforts, he constructs a bridge connecting the layered imagery in Brooks's verse, drawn from Black America.

Excavating the foundation of her poetic project, Harper strategically deploys Brooks's own words to direct and instruct the poem's fifth and final stanza. He returns to Brooks's title/phrase/image, "IN THE MECCA":

> And IN THE MECCA we could,
> and that narrative, sorrow songs
> for the marathon of your committal
> The prizes in our hands were your words. (262)

In this way, the poet examines Brooks's verse and the space(s) that it creates, proclaiming it to be inhabitable; it houses "that narrative" where Great Migration and the African Diaspora converge. Locating the intersection of these two outsized terms, Harper identifies connections between Brooks's poetry and the "sorrow songs," effectively recognizing their shared capacity to sustain and nourish Black America. Harper identifies Brooks's efforts to collect, protect, and preserve Black expressive culture as "the marathon of your committal" (262).

In the final line of "Wizardry," the poet returns to the markers that brought him to this point in the first place: "The prizes in our hands were your words" (262). Harper recalls and embraces the "I/we," "individual/collective" binaries that he explores in "Introducing the Blues." In this essay, Harper writes, "A reading list is also a good record player" before stating: "Black expression demands that people *do*—that people create themselves—that process is dynamic, that *both/and* is always better than *either/or*. . . . The poets here struggle as musicians to master the techniques necessary to carry the tunes of the people. The blues says *yes* to life. 'I' is always understood as we" (19, emphasis in original). With this account of the dynamics informing Black expressive culture and its audiences, Harper addresses the powerful force that Black artists bring to Black America. He identifies a set of psalm-like contradictions that he sees embedded in the foundation of Black expressive culture.

Harper's poetic engagements with Brooks makes connections with Sandra Jackson-Opoku's essay, "We Remember Sunday: Portrait of the Artist as an Ancestor." Like Harper, Jackson-Opoku recognizes Brooks capacity to say "yes" and her understanding of the close connection between the "I" and the "we" informing relationships between Black artists and their audiences. In this piece from *Revise the Psalm,* Jackson-Opoku points out that Brooks "created her work against the clamor of critics who warned that 'if being a Negro is the only subject, the writing is not important,' . . . [Brooks] knew Negroes are important and demonstrated this through the ordinary heroism, the complex challenges, and the sometimes terrible truths of living in the hurt of our Black skin . . . Gwendolyn Brooks burst the seams of straightjacketed stereotypes to give us a universe of full, flawed, and complicated characters. She made us see the drylongso, the everyday wonder of Old Marrieds and the Bean Eaters. She let us know the Bronzeville Boys and Girls, the Annie Allens, the Sadies and Maudes. She gave us Emmett Till, DeWitt Williams and Satin Legs Smith" (348). Jackson-Opoku's reading of Brooks verse locates additional points of intersection and convergence between Harper's discussion of Brooks's legacy within Black letters and American poetry writ large. These links also become evident in "Zen: The *Trainride* Home to the Welcome Table," an elegy of Brooks's life and work included in *Use Trouble.*

"*Trainride*" (which bears the epigraph "In Memory of Gwendolyn Brooks, 1917–2000") begins with the poet quickly establishing a dialogue concerned with death, departure, homegoing, and loss as the poem. Harper opens with a pair of unrhymed couplets:

> We know you parsed your best and worst thoughts
> on the train

> so this is traintalk.
> the waiters are weeping
> (in the chair car your baggage is at parade rest) (118)

Over the poem's fifteen couplets and three enjambed triplets, "*Trainride*" collects the set of loose threads comprising the literary dialogue and personal engagements the poet maintained with his literary champion. For example, when Harper states "HOLD ON" in the first line of the poem's sixth couplet, the poem returns to the dynamic he explores in "Wizardry," signaled by his use of Brooks's words with uppercase letters. At the same time, the poet extends the connective, reflective sensibility of "*Trainride*" using the parenthetical line that follows, "(I remember the whole family at lunch in Providence Plantations)," to complete the couplet. The poet effectively constructs a high poetic pedestal for Brooks to occupy: "arpeggio daughter of the sacred elements on our periodic table/ mother of the exquisite phrase break our hearts with every heartwork" (119).

To extend this deep riff on the "poetic saga of song," the poet identifies foundational elements of Brooks's poetic project. For instance, in the eleventh stanza of "*Trainride*," Harper confirms Brooks's praiseworthiness:

> yes, you were a "friendship train" in the argot of motown
> so glorious the pen (and handwriting) as none other than our holy ghost
>   champeen (119)

Discussing Brooks in these terms, Harper joins Jackson-Opoku in characterizing the elder poet as a literary pioneer, capable of breaking those "straightjacketed stereotypes" he sees engulfing both the lived experience and representation of Black Artists.

Connecting the poet and her work to "the ancestors" in this way, Harper locates their presence at "the welcome table." Having arrived at this destination, categorizing the circumstances of this journey as "Gwendolynian," the poet identifies the unfolding conditions as occurring within "the extreme unction of this tabernacletrain." He cites the elements of this environment—"tight quarters of the kitchenette on wheels," and "those . . . soothe as the songbirds strutting on air"—in terms that recall those segments of Black America mapped by Brooks. Parenthetically imploring his spirit guide into the literary word to "(look homeward angel just a little ahead of the curve)," "*Trainride*" comes to its conclusion. In the poem's last two stanzas, Harper delivers a riff on Sterling A. Brown's "No Hiding Place" before directing "GWEN" to go home:

> Went down to the place to hide my face
> (there's no hiding place down here)

   on the levee   with the angels   to spread those gorgeous wings:
   Zen   GWEN   key to the zone of understanding as universe the poet
      contemplate (119)

"*Trainride*" stands as another of Harper's "made connections," binding poet and subject, poet and poet, poet and audience, drawing from twin pools of overwhelming joy and unbearable sorrow, flowing simultaneously both to and from the psalms.

Epilogue

". . . Every Goodbye Ain't Gone"

Along with his duties as poet, teacher, scholar, editor, and cultural conservator, Michael S. Harper also served as a faithful correspondent, passing news,
information, and advice to a wide circle of individuals, whom he referred to as
"the people on my list." Using an array of communication tools to deliver these
messages, his "adaptive use" of landline telephones, voice mail, fax machines,
email, and cell phones frequently brought smiles and raised eyebrows among
his correspondents. Away from these experiments in communications, the majority of Harper's dispatches were sent out through the United States Postal
Service on 3" x 5" manila cardstock as "post cards."

Filled corner-to-corner with typewritten updates, instructions, and encouragement, Harper's post cards arrived regularly in the mailboxes of his intended
receivers. Even as email became his primary mode of communication in the
early 1990s, he sent out dozens of these missives each week. His correspondents
recall the rate and volume at which these personalized messages were produced
as well as their uncanny sense of timing. A particular post card might bring
attention to current or future events and circumstances that Harper understood
as consequential. For example, in a post card dated January 20, 2001, he considers the presidential inauguration of George W. Bush:

> now viewing panorama of inauguration, changeover, including
> demonstrators in cspan (sic); asking myself the 'proper rhetoric/
> for power, presidential and other, as nation digests its inhabitants
> ala (sic) WCWms: "history for us begins with murder and enslavement,

not with discovery;" and marveling how amnesia is always selective
and ubiquitous, simultaneously, when command is stirred by
"selective" memory, as the nation staggers toward a "perfection" of
itself; euphemism upon euphemism: (Harper 1–20 01 postcard)

Harper explains that "when I was younger . . . I parsed my sense of timing in
the US Post Office, in Airmail, for a way of telling this 'native ground story.'"
He ends with this: "enjoyed (our) visit to ritual ground, Harper's Ferry and the
many psychic confluences" (Harper 1 20 01 postcard). This message is just one
example of the hundreds (thousands?) of direct dispatches that Harper would
send out in a year.

Not surprisingly, as Harper used email more frequently, his rate of post
card production decreased. However, during this transition he continued to
use the United State Postal Service to send out large envelopes, stuffed with
photocopies of essays, interviews, poems, newspaper clippings, and other items
that he understood to be of interest to people on 'the list." Like the post cards,
the materials he passed along in these mailings were "forward looking." These
"packages," in effect, anticipated developments and delivered instructions that
were to be taken up at the right moment. For example, in a message dated No-
vember 26, 1994, written on a piece of note paper from the Yaddo artist's colony, Harper writes that he is "struggling with HONERABLE AMENDMENTS (sic),
a new book of poems, overdue at press." He adds that he recently obtained an
audio recording of the proceedings at Ralph Ellison's Memorial Service, which
took place in Manhattan during the spring. Along with this note, the package
also included a copy of *Clerestory*, volume XII.

The table of contents for this volume of *"Brown/ RISD journal of the arts"*
includes contributions from a list of artists whose careers were, at the time,
in their formative stages. For example, this *Clerestory* number features works
by electronic musician Tara Rogers, film maker Talia Hadid, and painter Jim
Drain, along with poems by Rosa Alcala Diaz, Prageeta Sharma, and Arron
Kunin in addition to fiction from Jean Tay and Betsy Boyd. The volume also
includes poems by Kevin Young,[1] whose first volume, *Most Way Home,* was
selected by Lucille Clifton for publication in the National Poetry Series that
fall. Away from the promise of its contributors, however, at the top right-hand
corner of the page, a hand-written note, bearing the initials "MSH," states,
"Michael—see p 33."

Further down on the volume's table of contents, beneath his name and
the titles of his two contributions to *Clerestory* XII—"Thimble" and "Par-
enting"—Harper left a miniscule checkmark beside the name "Rachel Maria
Harper," his daughter, whose poem "The Giant Speaks" also appears in the

volume. Found on page thirty-three and arriving with the italicized dedication *"for my father,"* this poem delivers a set of first-hand observations of Harper. Through its eleven quatrains, the younger Harper examines some of the work her father performed on the Brown University campus:

> He stands at the podium
> clearing his throat
> in a custom-made wool suit
> size 54 Long.
> The room is filled
> with his students:
> white women who've
> read *Invisible Man* and
>
> memorized "Phenomenal Woman"
> (at the request of his syllabus)
> but cannot find the portrait of
> Inman Page in the library foyer.
>
> He does not look
> for his color
> in this crowd
> they do not go to poetry
>
> readings (or jazz clubs)
> to experience their culture;
> history is the only reference
> they cite in their bibliography.
>
> So he reads to the
> ones who listen
> and writes for the
> ones who don't.
>
> Towering over parents
> at the reception, he speaks
> to let them know that
> 350 lbs is not wasted
>
> off a football field
> and that silence
> can never be
> a proper apology.

And even though
their behavior doesn't
warrant any favors
he saves an autograph

for the no shows,
and will write their
recommendations
when the time comes.

A reward for saying Du Bois
and for knowing how
to refuse watermelon
with a smile. (Rachel Harper, "The Giant Speaks," 33)

Recognizing Harper as a Black man, Black writer, and Black faculty member, "The Giant Speaks" captures a sense of the outsized imprint that the poet's presence and persona made on the Brown campus during his five decades of employment (1971–2015) at the university.

Rachel Harper's poem simultaneously connects and differentiates between the poet, his work, and place of employ. She bears witness to the combination of professional service, teaching, and artistry that her father brought to the Brown community. Drawing on experiences and observations, made both at home and at the university (where she studied as an undergraduate from 1990 to 1994), the poet constructs "The Giant Speaks" as both a father/daughter poem and an inside view of the terms and conditions binding a prominent Black poet to an elite American university. In this way, Michael Harper's movements and actions map the color line, tracing its contours both on and away from the Brown campus. In this portrait of her father, the poet presents the elder Harper advocating for his students and vigilantly monitoring the campus climate.

Marking intersections between Harper's personal and professional life, "The Giant Speaks" gestures to strategic adaptations that the poet made in his approach to the framework of the institution and its conventions. Rachel Harper's poem captures the complexity of the roles Michael Harper took on in the classroom, within the English Department, and as a university figure. The poem takes stock of the impact Brown University made on the poet's project, presenting candid snapshots of the poet entering the latter phases of his career. "The Giant Speaks" effectively previews the decidedly local orientation assumed by the verse found in Harper's *Honorable Amendments*.

Published shortly after his daughter's poem appeared in *Clerestory XII*, the Brown community servess as both source and resource for several poems found in *Honorable Amendments*. For example, "The Ghost of Soul Making, "dedicated to long-serving English Department administrative assistant Ruth Oppenheim, and "Mr. Knowelton Predicts," written for Daniel G. Knowlton, bookbinder at Brown's John Hay Library are two of many poems that bring attention Harper's ties to campus life. Similarly, "Manog: Angola" composed for Harper's friend and colleague, Professor Anani Dzidzenyo, also appears in the volume; as does "Testifying," dedicated to the memory of Dean Harriet W. Sheridan. More poems written for and about the Brown community are published in Harper's *Use Trouble,* including "Good Bye to All That," written for Bernard Bruce, first Black dean of Brown's Graduate School, and "Public Letter: Visible Ink," a poem dedicated to Howard W. Swearer, the university's fifteenth president (1977–88).

In these and other occasional works from his later volumes, the poet provides a sketch the Brown community at the turn of the twentieth century. These works are supplemented by poems that were not widely circulated, like "Boutonniere," dedicated to the memory of English Professor Elmer M. Blistein, and "Beauty Shell," a memorial tribute Harper wrote for Bernice Clarke Lewis, dedicated to her son, Dean Bernard Bruce Sr. Although the numerous discussions of his workplace and portraits of his co-workers have not received a great deal of critical attention, they include engagements with familiar subjects such as kinship, history, and Black music. Throughout these elegies and praise poems, Harper articulates his pursuit of the aesthetic and spiritual nexus that his work articulates as "A LOVE SUPREME."

In addition to opening discussions of Harper's Brown poems, "The Giant Speaks" also provides context for other verse published during the later stages of the poet's career. When Rachel Harper's poem appeared in *Clerestory XII,* Michael Harper had recently completed his term as Poet Laureate for the State of Rhode Island and Providence Plantations. Serving as the Ocean State's first poet laureate from 1989–93, the elder Harper produced public, commemorative, and occasional works for official events conducted by his adoptive home state, and several of these works were published in *Honorable Amendments*. Appearing in the "Laureate Notes" section of the volume, these titles include "Rhode Island (SSBNT740): A Toast," written for the christening of the USS *Rhode Island,* as well as "Madam Tutu" and "Mule," two poems dedicated to Alberto Torres Pereira, a Providence community organizer from the Fox Point neighborhood, who served as consultant at the State Library of Rhode Island and primary investigator for Rhode Island College's Cape

Verdean Oral History Project. In these pieces, along with other Rhode Island poems written at this time, Harper maintains his project's well-developed sense of temporal and geographic space. These qualities are fully evident, for example, in "Laureate Notes," the title piece from the eponymously titled section of *Honorable Amendments,* in which Harper demonstrates the full-contact, no-holds barred, approach to literary engagement that he enacted as Rhode Island's poet laureate.

The poem, dedicated *"to the Providence Journal,"* delivers a scathing editorial message to "the ProJo," Rhode Island's principal news source during the twentieth century. "Laureate Notes" excoriates the political, cultural, and social orientation of the Ocean State's newspaper of record. Harper assembles a set of "notes" he's taken in various capacities that include citizen, father, Black man, and Rhode Island poet laureate. Proclaiming that "Four papers a day, *Globe, Times,* /*Monitor,* are not enough," he states that the poem "is a personal editorial" (75). By locating the intersections of identity, geography, and history, "Laureate Notes" moves along the pathways that Harper blazed throughout the course of his career and during his time in Rhode Island.

For example, in the poem's opening stanza, Harper's speaker informs the paper's editors that it's time to "Update your Photo/ gallery." Critiquing the manner in which people of color appear in the paper's photos—underexposed, with their features distorted by ink—he writes:

> . . . all black people do not
> appear in the negative and in broad
> daylight, let's say on Broad Street,
> a rainbow, a cliché but full range
> of coloration. (75)

Broad Street is the main thoroughfare in South Providence, the city's largest Black and Latinx neighborhood. Harper excoriates the newspaper for ignoring Providence's diversity. In the second stanza, Harper's speaker continues his indictment of the newspaper: "please give us the facts: save the attitudes for the collection plate." Shifting the focus of the poem in its third stanza, the poet states:

> Your police news lack how you treat
> the rich, how you make fun of
> immigrants, who count their
> change in the women's room,
> which is often out of paper
> this the paper of the numbers
> this is the paper of the rich. (75)

Delivering these images in this stacked tower of signification, the poet addresses the newspaper's failure to engage unresolved issues relating to corruption, gender, ethnicity, and inequality in the city. To make his concern for the newspaper's orientation evident, Harper considers its coverage of crime and the city's police force. In this way, the poet accuses "the Projo" of wrapping its readership, along with the city's government, in so much "paper."

The poet intensifies his tone in the fourth stanza of "Laureate Notes": "I will not comment on the police: /they are brown, sometimes on horses, and often patrol" (76). In addition to referencing the color of the uniforms worn by officers of the Providence police department (PPD) and gesturing toward members of its mounted command, Harper suggests that the Ocean State's paper of record is either unwilling or unable to investigate questions relating to PPD actions. Eschewing the impulse to editorialize, instead, the poet follows up on this articulate "no comment" statement by offering reportage from the field. Endeavoring to deliver "just the facts," Harper writes:

> my boy watched you chase
> a 15-year-old up Chestnut Street
> in a heisted car, and, when he lost
> control watched him beaten into
> submission, and because he was upstairs,
> and not at ground level,
> with a perfect view for justice,
> and my answer, which came quickly
> because he stutters, looks Cape Verdean,
> has been hassled by men in brown
> for their amusement. (76)

With matters of family, identity, geography, and race converging in this passage, Harper effectively goes "on record," identifying the ongoing struggle for just and equitable living conditions within his neighborhood, the city of Providence, and throughout Rhode Island.

The poem turns away from these overtly political subjects, addressing issues of a more intimate or personal nature in the fifth stanza of "Laureate Notes":

> I realize these men have their own children;
> I realize they are not in love with mine;
> when it comes to the protection, editors,
> one must get one's blows in early,
> if you want to make sense
> to a kid about justice,
> about the law. (76)

Harper extends his engagement with a both/and impulse. Redoubling his exploration of Black life and American experience in his poetic project, he observes the color line, marking its sharp edges and blunt angles. Engaging a double-edged, "peculiar twoness," Harper traces the shape of justice in a city where the PPD and the ProJo walk their respective beats.

Surveying matters of family, law, and belonging, Harper identifies how the city's systemic realities become translated as "tough lessons" delivered through "schools of hard knocks." With the poet discussing this established order in terms of "protection" and "editors," he suggests that he and his eldest son have witnessed the power of these forces at their point of convergence. As such, "Laureate Notes" delivers a honed and detailed close reading of the interplay between public information (the newspaper) and public service (the police) in Providence. The poem echoes Harper's work in "American History," his poetic master study of Du Boisian double consciousness and Ellisonian notions of ethical schizophrenia and historical amnesia in the United States, published in *Dear John, Dear Coltrane*.

Harper continues his exegetic explication of this system of distortion and double standards as the poem enters its sixth stanza. Clarifying his terms and marking the direction and movement of this power flow, the poet writes:

> This is one or two incidents,
> it must stand from the whole;
> it is all he knows about order.
> it is all he knows about law. (76)

These lines effectively acknowledge the refraction and doubling that transpires on or along the color line in Providence. Merging with narratives concerning the car, the cops, and the fifteen-year-old, these conclusions become a backdrop for the Black poet and his son to make sense of their city. They process the ambiguity of implied details and acknowledge that these "one or two incidents," in turn, "must stand for the whole." At the same time, the poet acknowledges that this conclusion is not an end in and of itself. With "the whole" becoming "all he knows about order," the unnamed male referenced in this line—whether it is understood as the fifteen-year-old youth, the poet's son, or poet himself—is a person of color, whose city and state have delivered a clear message "about law" and his status with respect to it.

The underlying impact of these inequities are underscored in the final stanza of "Laureate Notes" as the poet concludes his literary letter to the editor:

> Tomorrow: car theft; tomorrow: trash
> collection; tomorrow: judges and juries;

> tomorrow IRS, BVA, MLA PAL, CVS, NBC, BRU
> tomorrow: happened today. (76)

The "car theft" and any news reports about the incident and its movements through the legal system, including "judges and juries," are poised, ready to find their way into the ink and newsprint of "tomorrow" as headlines and subheadings. Harper generates a list of terms that arrive as destined certainties—as predictable and regular as the "trash/ collection"—that also comes "tomorrow." As these terms assemble in the poem, they form a regimented order that constructs a predictable future. Serving as a set of cryptic signifiers, they reference a consolidation of power and guided certainties, advancing objectives that the newspaper and the police department fashion into "law" and "order."

By the poem's penultimate line, the shape that this "tomorrow" will take is reduced to a blurring string of abbreviations. While some of these acronyms are immediately recognizable to most readers—for example, "IRS" (Internal Revenue Service), "MLA" (Modern Language Association), "NBC" (National Broadcast Company), CVS (Rhode Island–based pharmacy giant, originally known as "Consumer Value Stores")—others, such as "BRU," "BVA," and "PAL" are less familiar. Through his decision to use these abbreviations, Harper deploys enigmatic or double-edged references as a foundation of his poetic project. Examining these ambiguous acronyms and probing them for possible references offers insight into both the poem and its relationship to the poet's body of work.

Beginning with BRU—the widely accepted shorthand for the call letters of WBRU-95.5, a Providence radio station, formerly affiliated with Brown University—it becomes possible to understand the poet as making an "obscure" reference that audiences either recognize as a result of "prior knowledge" or require additional information in order to interpret more completely. At the same time, however, both BVA and PAL present a set of meanings with a broader range of interpretive possibilities. How these acronyms are understood influences the meaning of the poem. For example, if PAL is understood to stand for "Police Athletic League," "Laureate Notes" maintains one set of valences. If, instead, it is understood as the abbreviation for "Phase Alternating Line"—a type of color information associated with video playback or television broadcast—it carries another. Both readings hold interpretive relevance. The first because the poem is about police and their efforts at community outreach; the second is poignant given the commentary "Laureate Notes" delivers through the poet's discussion of the *Providence Journal's* visual depictions of Black and Brown people, presented in the poem's first stanza.

Similarly, BVA holds a complex range of possible interpretations. It may be understood as making reference to the "Board of Veteran's Appeals," the deliberative branch of the Veteran's Administration, which conveys a particular governmental and bureaucratic orientation. However, if it is understood to stand for "boundary value analysis" (a term associated with "equivalence partitioning theory," a software creation application), the poem engages a set of technocratic associations, involving black box testing methods. A third interpretive possibility emerges if the acronym is understood to reference an international marketing and research consultancy group known as "BVA," which specializes in "reinforcing persuasive strategies," "improving the effectiveness of public policies," and "the fundamentals of behavioral economics and nudging" (BVA-group.com).

This constellation of possible interpretations extends into the poem's final line: "tomorrow: happened today" (76), which effectively concludes the poem's survey of Providence, Rhode Island, and its landscapes of power. Assembling and arranging a disparate collection of signals and signs, the poet issues a challenge calling for a change and revisions for his city and state's intrenched cultural configurations. He does so, working through a series of improvised arrangements within the familiar modes of convergent history and generative kinship. The poem and its speaker effectively deliver this hard-edged critique of the *Providence Journal*'s "consistency," demonstrating Harper's poetic project as working to disturb the peace. Acknowledging this impulse and its capacity to inform and connect Harper's body of work to his audience, the poet speaks its truths and sing its songs. I leave him there.

NOTES

Chapter 1—Understanding Michael S. Harper

1. According to a US Housing and Urban Development report, "Homeownership: Separate and Unequal, 1940–2006," homeownership among Black Americans in 1940 was 22.8 percent, about half the rate of white American homeownership at the time (Leigh and Huff, "Homeownership"). Linda Dynan writes that in 1930, there were 3,770 Black physicians in the United States, who accounted for 0.025 percent of the 153,803 physicians in the country. The total number of Black physicians rose to 3,810 by 1940, but this represented only 0.022 percent of the 175,163 physicians in the country "The Impact of Medical Education Reform," 246).

Chapter 2—Acknowledgment (Kinship)

1. Stepto's reading of "Grandfather" attributes the maxim to Brown, recognizing it as one of eight cryptic epigraphs Harper includes in *Nightmare Begins Responsibility*. The aphorism speaks to a no-nonsense, stoic sensibility that Harper identifies as a common thread in a kinship line connecting Brown, Gwendolyn Brooks, and the poet's father, Warren W. Harper, among others.

2. Harper's connection to Black music, particularly jazz, is central to critical considerations of his verse. Innovative Black musician John Coltrane maintains a prominent place in Harper's poetic project. Presenting Coltrane as an artist and kinsman, the poet establishes the musician's significance within his body of work. Harper repeatedly draws on the phrase "*a love supreme*," using it to punctuate the realization of kinship bonds. Coltrane chants the phrase in "Acknowledgement," the opening section of his suite "A Love Supreme." Coltrane composed and recorded the piece with McCoy Tyner (piano), Paul Chambers (bass), and Elvin Jones (drums), members of his so-called "Classic Quartet," on December 9, 1964. The recording was released by Impulse in January 1965.

3. The "anthem" referenced by Harper's speaker is arguably Coltrane's "Alabama," which opens with a six-note broken arpeggio. In his interview with Abraham Chapman, Harper suggests that Coltrane formulated the composition's melody while "riding a train from New York to Philadelphia, possibly reading a newspaper account of Martin Luther King's eulogy for four Black girls blown up in a Birmingham church in 1963" (Chapman, "An Interview with Michael S. Harper," 466).

4. Harper includes a prose section entitled "Notes on Forms and Fictions" as an afterword to *Songlines in Michaeltree: New and Collected Poems*. Discussing his sense of the volume and its project, the poet writes, "the title of this book . . . is meant to

demarcate the early lessons I learned in Brooklyn, New York, as a child" (371). At the outset of collection, the poet explains his understanding of the "songline" as an approximation of an indigenous Australian principle that gained broader English usage after the publication of Bruce Chatwin's work of creative nonfiction, *The Songlines*. Chatwin's account of life in the Australian outback and the struggle for aboriginal land rights regards songlines to be "the labyrinth of invisible pathways which meander all over Australia" (2).

5. The version of "Last Affair: Bessie's Blues Song" found in *Song: I Want a Witness* (and the revised edition of *Debridement*) consists of four, six-line stanzas. An alternate version of the poem, initially published in *Images of Kin: New and Collected Poems*, uses "Bessie's song" as a chorus. This seven-stanza, multivoice "duet" has become the more widely discussed, more familiar version of the poem.

6. Alice Walker's essay, "In Search of Zora Neale Hurston," chronicles the writers attempt during the summer of 1973 to locate Hurston's unmarked burial site. While seeking information about the final years of Hurston's life, Walker claimed to be the departed writer's "niece." Walker's successful efforts to honor Hurston's contributions to Black culture culminated in the placement of a black stone marker on Hurston's burial site bearing the epitaph: "ZORA NEALE HURSTON; 'A GENIUS OF THE SOUTH'; 1901–1960; NOVELIST, FOLKLORIST; ANTHROPOLOGIST."

7. Harper's *Nightmare Begins Responsibility* includes a poem entitled "Alice Braxton Johnson," dedicated to the maternal grandmother he references in these lines from "Alice."

8. Harper organized Brown University's The Ralph Ellison Festival in September 1979. The festival featured presentations of scholarly and creative work, produced in conversation with Ellison and his novel *Invisible Man* as well as remarks by the author. Materials from festival were published in "Celebrating Ellison," special volume of the *Carleton Miscellany*. The collection includes poems by Harper; essays by John Wright, Robert Stepto, and Melvin Dixon; and Ellison's "Going to the Territory."

9. In his "Preface to *The Book of American Negro Poetry*," James Weldon Johnson discusses dialect poetry and—by extension—the minstrel tradition as "instrument with two full stops, pathos and humor." Ellison famously describes the blues in his essay "Richard Wright's Blues" as "an impulse to keep the painful details and episodes of a brutal experience alive in one's aching consciousness, to finger its jagged grain, and to transcend it, not by the consolation of philosophy but by squeezing from it a near-tragic, near-comic lyricism" through its "autobiographical chronicle of personal catastrophe expressed lyrically" (78–79).

Chapter 3—Resolution (History as Mode)

1. Professor Callahan has served as Ellison's literary executor since the novelist died in April 1994. He oversaw the preparation of *Juneteenth*, Ellison's posthumously published novel, in addition to publishing works on Black literature and twentieth-century American literature. He is Morgan S. Odell Professor of Humanities at Lewis and Clark College.

2. Recognizing the poet's interest in what Ralph Ellison calls "American unwritten history" allows readers of "American History" to consider that Francis Scott Key's poem "Defense of Fort M'Henry" includes four stanzas, not typically sung as part of the US national anthem. Slaves and matters related to slavery arise in the third stanza, where Key writes: "And where is that band who so vauntingly swore / That the havoc of war

and the battle's confusion / A home and a country should leave us no more? / Their blood has wash'd out their foul foot-steps' pollution, / No refuge could save the hireling and slave, / From the terror of flight or the gloom of the grave." Available at Library of Congress website, https://www.loc.gov/item/ihas.100010457/.

3. Several accounts recap Harper's rise to prominence in American letters. Anthony Walton assembles what is perhaps the most succinct version of the story in "The Hard-headed Romantic," published in *Brown Alumni Monthly*.

4. Born in 1776 on a Henrico County, Virginia, tobacco plantation, Gabriel Prosser lived as an enslaved person of African descent from the time of the War for American Independence through the early national period. Gabriel was literate and a trained blacksmith. Assisted by his brothers Solomon and Martin, Gabriel organized an uprising of enslaved people living in and around Richmond during the spring and summer of 1800. Storms passed through the city on the day of the uprising, interfering with the execution of their plan and leading to the capture of Gabriel and his brothers. They were among twenty-three people sentenced to hang for taking part in the uprising.

5. In line fourteen of "History as Bandages: Polka Dots and Moonbeams" the poet uses the word "Squaw," bringing the poem into conversations concerning the origins and use of this word. The word likely gained its place in English as a disambiguation of an Algonquin language group root word, used variously to reference women. It acquired derogatory connotations when used by Anglo-Europeans in reference to indigenous women, dating back to the seventeenth-century as British colonists claimed the territories that are known as "New England." The racist, sexist connotations of the word are widely acknowledged, due in large part to work performed by poet Joy Harjo (Mvskoke) in the 1990s.

6. Michael S. Harper and Shirley Buffington Harper divorced in 1998 after twenty-seven years of marriage, during which they witnessed the births of five children, three who survived into adulthood and two who died within hours of their arrival. All of their children hold a place within the poet's conception of the family. Harper's volume *Debridement* illustrates this situation. The volume is dedicated to all five of the Harper's children: Rolland Warren Harper, Patrice Cuchulain Harper, and Rachel Maria Harper are referred to as "the living," and Ruben Massai and Michael Steven Jr. are called "the dead/ torn away." Harper's work includes numerous poems dedicated to and/or written for each of his living children. "Welcome" and "Forty: 6.28.06" are dedicated to Rolland. "Love Medley: Patrice Cuchulain" and "Portrait of a Son at Rhinebeck Train Station" are for Patrice. "Blackjack," "Eve (Rachel)," and "Crossing Lake Michigan" are written to Rachel. The poet's explorations of his two late sons' brief lives have received much critical attention and discussion. These deeply personal excavations found in poems such as "Ruben, Ruben," "Deathwatch" and "Nightmare Begins Responsibility" shaped reception and understanding of Harper's poetic project.

7. In 2001 Harper oversaw the publication of *Debridement: Song: I Want a Witness & Debridement* with Paradigm Press. Working in collaboration with poet Ben Lerner, at the time a Brown University undergraduate, and receiving assistance from Donn and Temple Nelson of Lost Roads Publishers, Harper collected poems from two previously published volumes of verse, *Song: I Want a Witness* and *Debridement*, combining them into a revised edition of *Debridement,* as he had conceived of the project over thirty years earlier. Anthony Walton's introduction to the collection describes the volume as "a miracle, or two or three" (11), praising its exploration of "larger history and belief system[s]"(13). In addition to assisting Harper bring about his original vision for these

poems, Lerner also produced *To Cut Is to Heal,* a critical companion to the revised volume, which includes an in-depth interview with Harper about the project.

8. Harper's "Photographs: Negatives" cycle collects imagery from time the poet's family spent in Dighton, Massachusetts, a Bristol County town where the Harper family held property. During the colonial period, portions of present-day southeastern Massachusetts, including Bristol County, were claimed by the British Empire and administered as the Plymouth Colony. Established in 1620 by William Bradford, this territory is renowned as the site of the First Thanksgiving and steeped in what Ellison calls "American mythic history." This portion of present-day Massachusetts is referred to as "the Old Colony." The name recalls the establishment of the "Old Colony Line," differentiating the Plymouth Colony from the Massachusetts Bay Colony, formed by Governor Winthrop in 1628. The Old Colony Line remained in place until both colonies were united as the Province of Massachusetts Bay in 1691.

9. A 2015 National Parks Service post entitled "The Tree Root that Ate Roger Williams" states: "In 1860, the people of Providence decided to create a suitable memorial to the founder of Rhode Island. Community leaders went in search of Williams's remains. [Excavating the site where they believed Williams to be buried] . . . they found only nails, teeth, and bone fragments. They also found an apple tree root. The tree root looked as if it had taken on the form of Roger Williams. It had traveled the length of Williams's body, splitting at the hips, bending at the knees and turning up at the feet. Since 1860 the Rhode Island Historical Society has cared for this special tree root as representative of Rhode Island's founder and has had it on display in the John Brown House since 2007."

10. Pitcher Bob Gibson and outfielder Curt Flood were from the generation of Black baseball players that followed Jackie Robinson's integration of the Major Leagues in 1947. As teammates on the St. Louis Cardinals from 1959–1969, Flood and Gibson won three National League pennants (1964, 1967, 1968) and claimed World Series titles in '64 and '67. Outfielder Reggie Jackson and pitcher Vida Blue were in the next generation of Black major leaguers. Like Gibson and Flood, Blue and Jackson were teammates, playing on the Oakland Athletics in the 1970s, winners of three straight World Series from 1972–74.

Chapter 4—Pursuance (Black Music)

1. In "From Black to Blues," Andrews presents possibilities for understanding the blues and other blues-rooted musical forms as a foundation for analyzing Black expression. Building on work by LeRoi Jones (Amiri Baraka) on Black music and cultural products, such as *Blues People,* Andrews discusses blues-rooted music as a means of Black "self-empowerment," suggesting that it is, at once, "overlooked" and "the most significant of all the probable African adaptations/ retentions in African-American music."

2. The "Jazz Age" is typically associated with the "Hot Jazz" and "Roaring Twenties" along with the dynamic economic, social, and cultural transformations that occurred in United States after World War I. Its excesses and urgencies are often explored with respect to the Prohibition era (1920–33) and F. Scott Fitzgerald's fiction. It is also possible to discuss the proliferation of innovative jazz styles emerging between 1943 and 1968 as a second phase of the "Jazz Age." Black music in the mid-twentieth century is marked by a period of experimentation that produced a broad range of jazz styles, from Bebop to Cool to Free Jazz. It also involves the development of novel distribution

methods that include recording forms, concerts, festivals, specialty radio shows, and creative and journalistic literature.

3. In his autobiographical essay, "Every Shut Eye Ain't Sleep," Harper describes his Iowa M.A. thesis as a set of "improvised monologues." He adds that "they were terrible," but "the best I could do." The essay also relates the story behind the title of his thesis. Harper recalls sharing a live-work space with poet Lawson Inada in Iowa City. He suggests that the wall separating their rooms was so thin that they were able to spin LPs for one another. According to Harper, Inada was so enamored with side one of the Miles Davis's "Kind of Blue," that he wouldn't flip the LP, fearing that the album's second side would disappoint him; eventually Harper felt compelled played the second side of the album. Intrigued by what he was hearing through their thin wall, Inada knocked on Harper's door to ask about the "new music" that was playing. Harper responded, holding up the "Kind of Blue" album cover and saying, "Side two." "Hence," Harper writes, "the title of my thesis, 'Blues and Laughter'" (8).

4. Allan Morrison's 1953 article in *Ebony* magazine, "Can a Musician Return from the Brink of Insanity," reports that Art Tatum spoke to Richard Powell between sets to criticize his use of the left hand. Powell responded to Tatum's critique by soloing exclusively with the left hand when he returned to his piano for the following set.

5. Harper published a revised version of this poem as "A Coltrane Poem: 9 23 98 (2)" in *Use Trouble*, which uses italics and bold font throughout the poem to indicate titles of Coltrane compositions and proper names, including musicians. These modifications distinguish the work from "A Coltrane Poem: 9 23 98," establishing it as an "alternate take." As such, the two poems offer insight into Harper's work with, in, and through the Coltrane mode.

6. Harper included a slightly modified version of this poem in *Use Trouble* (2009) under the title "Coltrane Notes on the Millennium 9 23 2000."

7. In "Driving the Big Chrysler," the poet asks: "What does Detroit have to give my music / as elk-miles distance into shoal lights / dashes at sunrise over Oakland."

8. Harper nurtured the careers of several notable Black writers and poets across multiple generations. In the 1970s, his students included Melvin Dixon, Gayl Jones, and Sherley Anne Williams. Afaa Michael Weaver and Anthony Walton were among a second wave during the 1980s. During the 1990s, he worked with Rowan Ricardo Phillips, Kevin Young, and to a limited extent, Duriel E. Harris.

9. Harper met Hayden on the poetry circuit in the 1970s; they cultivated a profound friendship, rooted in a rich poetic conversation and regular correspondence. Many of their letters are discussed in Xavier Nichols's "Robert Hayden and Michael S. Harper a Literary Friendship."

10. Christopher Buck's detailed discussion of Hayden's "[American Journal]" speaks to Harper's role in the publication of *American Journal*, in his essay "Robert Hayden's "[American Journal]": A Multidimensional Analysis." Harper also offers an account of his work with Hayden and their making of *American Journal* in his 2006 essay, "The Metaphysics of American Journal."

11. The prospect of honoring Inman Page, who had served as a principal in Oklahoma City's segregated public school system while Ralph Ellison was a student, was Harper's pretext for bringing the novelist to Providence for the Ellison Festival in 1979.

12. These titles may be understood as promotional strategies, employed by white publishers, marketing work by Black writers to "incredulous" white audiences.

13. In "Big Chrysler," "Camarillo" references the California State Psychiatric facility

where Charlie Parker was hospitalized from July 1946 to January 1947 after experiencing a psychotic episode in Los Angeles. When Parker was released from the facility, he recorded a composition entitled "Relaxin' at Camarillo." Harper's poem effectively connects the disappointment of Bird and Trane's Los Angeles experiences, recalling that shortly before his death in 1967, health concerns forced Coltrane to cancel a series of Los Angeles performances.

14. In his 1988 interview with Reginald Martin, Harper discusses "Dear John, Dear Coltrane" and states: "I'm sure you're familiar with Stephen Henderson's *Understanding the New Black Poetry* . . . [Henderson] paid me [a] terrific compliment by reading [my] 'Dear John' poem extremely closely. He's the only one who ever asked me if the beginning of 'Dear John' is a reference to Du Bois and Sam Hose [a Black man lynched in Coweta County, Georgia in 1899] and it is" ("Interview with Michael S. Harper," 443).

Chapter 5—Psalm (Memory and Remembrances)

1. See Eduardo Corral's poem "To Robert Hayden." Corral's volume *Slow Lighting* was the first work by a Latinx poet to be awarded the Yale Younger Poet Prize.

2. Jacob Lawrence taught at the University of Washington from 1970 until his retirement in 1986. He and his wife, painter Gwendolyn Knight Lawrence, made Seattle their home. Lawrence passed away in June 2000.

3. Originally conceived as a follow-up volume to *Southern Road, No Hiding Place* was rejected in the mid-1930s by editors at Harcourt and Brace.

4. In the "Prologue" of Ralph Ellison's *Invisible Man* (1952), the novel's unnamed narrator initiates the work's explorations into the question of history. He suggests that "contradiction is how the world moves." Explaining that its motion is "[n]ot like an arrow, but a boomerang," Ellison's narrator admonishes readers to "Beware of those who speak of the *spiral* of history; they're preparing a boomerang. Keep a steel helmet handy" (6).

5. Interview "The Writing Life," Howard County Poetry and Literary Society Roland Flint and Michael S. Harper, 1994. https://www.youtube.com/.

6. Harper's line references Brooks's experience at the Second Black Writers Conference, held at Fisk University in 1967, which the regards to as a "turning point" in her career. The context events and impact of the Fisk Conference is examined by Derik Smith in his essay, "Quarreling in the Movement: Robert Hayden's Black Arts Era."

Epilogue: ". . . Every Goodbye Ain't Gone"

1. These poems by Young would be published in *Ardency: A Chronicle of the Amistad Rebels*, recipient of the 2011 Before Columbus American Book Award.

WORKS CITED

Works by Michael S. Harper

Blues and Laughter. State University of Iowa, 1963.

Collected Poems of Sterling A. Brown. Harper Colophon, 1980.

Dear John, Dear Coltrane. Ilini Books Edition, University of Illinois Press, 1985.

Debridement. Doubleday, 1973.

Debridement: Song: I Want a Witness and Debridement. Introduction by Anthony Walton. Paradigm Press, 2000.

"Every Shut-Eye Ain't Asleep." In *A Community of Writers: Paul Engle and the Iowa Writers' Workshop,* edited by Robert Dana, 78–88. University of Iowa Press, 1999.

Healing Song for the Inner Ear. University of Illinois Press, 1985.

History Is Your Own Heartbeat, 2nd ed. University of Illinois Press, 1972.

Honorable Amendments. University of Illinois Press, 1995.

I Do Believe in People: Remembrances of W. Warren Harper 1915–2004. Effendi Press, 2005.

"An Integer is a Whole Number." In *After Winter: The Art and Life of Sterling A. Brown,* edited by John Edgar Tidwell and Steven C. Tracy, 273–84. Oxford, 2009.

"Introducing the Blues." *American Poetry Review* 7, no. 1 (1977): 19.

Images of Kin: New and Selected Poems. University of Illinois Press, 1977.

"My Poetic Technique and the Humanization of the American Audience." In *Black American Literature and Humanism,* edited by R. Baxter Miller, 27–32. University Press of Kentucky, 1981.

Nightmare Begins Responsibility. University of Illinois Press, 1975.

Song: I Want a Witness. University of Pittsburgh Press, 1972.

Songlines in Michaeltree: New and Collected Poems. University of Illinois Press, 2000.

Use Trouble. University of Illinois Press, 2009.

AS EDITOR

Harper, Michael S., and Robert Stepto, eds. *Chant of Saints.* University of Illinois Press. 1979.

RECORDINGS

Harper, Michael S., and Paul Austerlitz. *Our Book on Trane: The Yaddo Sessions,* Yaddo, Yaddo 1, 2004.

Secondary Sources

Alexander, Elizabeth. "I Am a Black Man: Michael Harper's Black Aesthetic." In *The Black Interior: Essays by Elizabeth Alexander*, 59–91. Grey Wolf Press, 2005.

Allen, Frank. "Review of *Healing Song for the Inner Ear*, by Michael S. Harper." *Library Journal* 109, no. 20 (1984): 2284.

Andrews, Dwight A. "From Black to Blues: Towards a Blues Aesthetic." In *The Blues Aesthetic: Black Culture and Modernism*, edited by Richard Powell, 37–42. Washington Project for the Arts. 1989.

Beavers, Herman. "Map of the Soothsayer." https://www.academia.edu/.

Benston, Kimberly W. "Harper and Trane: Modal Enactments of 'A Love Supreme.'" *Journal of Ethnic Literature*, no. 6 (2016): 38–60.

———. "Late Coltrane: A Re-Membering of Orpheus." In *Chant of Saints*, edited by Michael S. Harper and Robert Stepto, 413–24. University of Illinois Press, 1979.

Blunk, Jonathan. "Elective Kinship: Improvisations on Portraiture in the Poetry of Michael S. Harper." Michael S. Harper Symposium. March 15, 2013, Reynolds Alumni Center University of Missouri, Columbia.

Boorstin, Daniel. "Introduction upon Robert Hayden's Appointment as Consultant-in-Poetry." *Obsidian: Black Literature in Review* 8, no. 1 (1981): 16–18.

Corral, Eduardo C. "To Robert Hayden." https://www.poetryfoundation.org/poetry magazine/.

Callahan, John. "Testifying Voices in Michael Harper's *Images of Kin*," Review of *Images of Kin* by Michael S. Harper. *Black American Literary Forum* 13, no. 3 (1979): 89–92.

Chapman, Abraham. "An Interview with Michael S. Harper." *Arts in Society* 11, no. 1 (1974): 463–71.

Cooke, Michael G. *Afro-American Literature in the Twentieth Century: The Achievement of Intimacy*. Yale University Press, 1984.

Dodd, Elizabeth. "Another Version: Michael S. Harper, William Clark and the Problem of Historical Blindness." *Western American Literature* 33, no. 1 (1998), 60–72.

———. "The Rainbowed Swamp: History as Moral Ecology in the Poetry of Michael S. Harper." In *Beyond Nature Writing*, 177–94. Charlottesville: University of Virginia, 2001.

Dynan, Linda. "The Impact of Medical Education Reform on the Racial Health Status Gap, 1920–1930: A Difference-in-Differences Analysis." *Review of Black Political Economy* 34, no. 3–4 (2007): 245–58.

Ellison, Ralph. "Going to the Territory." In *Going to the Territory*, 120–45. Random House, 1986.

———. *Invisible Man*. Vintage Books Edition, 1972.

———. "Richard Wright's Blues." In *Shadow and Act*, 77–91. Vintage Books, 1972.

Flint, Roland. "Interview with Michael S. Harper, in "The Writing Life," Howard County Poetry and Literary Society, 1994. https://www.youtube.com/.

Harper, Rachel M. "The Giant Speaks." *Clerestory* 12 (1994): 33.

Harper, W. Warren. *I Am Katherine: A Memoir*. Self-published, 1995.

Henderson, Stephen E. *Understanding the New Black Poetry: Black Speech and Black Music as Poetic References*. William Morrow and Company, 1973.

Hirsch, Edward. "An Interview with Michael S. Harper." *Gulf Coast* 6, no. 1 (1993): 7–14.

Keegan, James R. "History, Heartbeat, and Jazz: An Interview with Michael S. Harper." *Caesura*, no. 7 (1987).

Johnson, James Weldon. *God's Trombones: Seven Negro Sermons in Verse.* Chapel Hill: University of North Carolina Library, 2004. Electronic edition, http://docsouth.unc.edu/southlit/johnson/johnson.html.

Leigh, Wilhelmina A., and Danielle Huff. "Separate and Unequal, 1940–2006," written for The Joint Center for Political and Economic Studies, Washington, DC, 2007. https://archives.lib.duke.edu/.

Lenz, Gunter. "Black Poetry and Black Music: History and Traditions: Michael Harper and John Coltrane." In *History and Tradition in Afro-American Culture,* edited by Gunter Lenz, 277–327. Campus Verlag, 1984.

Lerner, Ben. *To Cut Is to Heal.* Paradigm Press, 2000.

Lloyd, David. "Interview with Michael S. Harper." *TriQuarterly,* no. 65 (1986): 119–28.

Martin, Reginald. "Interview with Michael S. Harper." *Black American Literary Forum* 24, no. 3 (1990): 441–51.

National Park Service. "The Tree Root that Ate Roger Williams." Roger Williams National Memorial, Rhode Island. www.nps.gov/.

Nicholas, Xavier. "Robert Hayden and Michael S. Harper: A Literary Friendship." *Callaloo* 17, no. 4 (1994): 976–1018.

O'Brien, John. *Interviews with Black Writers.* Liveright, 1973.

Olds, Sharon. "Notes on Gwendolyn Brooks." In *Revise the Psalm: Work Celebrating the Writing of Gwendolyn Brooks,*" edited by Quraysh Ali Lansana and Sandra Jackson-Opoku, 262–64. Curbside Splendor Publishing, 2017.

Ostriker, Alicia. "Psalm and Anti-Psalm: A Personal View." *The American Poetry Review* 31, no. 4 (2002): 11–15.

Payne, J. R. Review of *Healing Song for Inner Ear. World Literature Today* 60, no. 1 (1986): 117.

Pope, Jacquelyn. "Citizen Pilgrim Poet." *Harvard Review,* no. 20 (2001): 52–54.

Rowell, Charles H. "'Down Don't Worry Me': An Interview with Michael S. Harper." *Callaloo* 13, no. 4 (1990): 780–800.

Seaman, Donna. "Review of *Use Trouble.*" *Booklist* 105, no 11 (2009): 22.

Smith, Derik. "Quarreling in the Movement: Robert Hayden's Black Arts Era." *Calloloo* 33, no. 2 (2010): 449–66.

Steiner, George. "On Difficulty." *Journal of Aesthetics and Art Criticism* 36, no. 3 (1978): 263–76.

Stepto, Robert B. "Michael S. Harper, Poet as Kinsman: The Family Sequence." *The Massachusetts Review* 17, no. 3 (1976): 477–502.

———. "Michael Harper's Extended Tree: John Coltrane and Sterling Brown." *The Hollins Critic* 13, no. 3 (1976): 1–16.

Treseler, Heather. "Office Hours: A Memoir and an Interview with Michael S. Harper." *Iowa Review* 39, no. 4 (2009–10): 100–123.

"Undaunted Pursuit of Fury." *Time.* April 6, 1970. https://content.time.com/time/.

Vollmer, Judith. "Weather, Sundials, and Other Time Machines in the Poetry of Michael S. Harper." Michael S. Harper Symposium. March 15, 2013, Reynolds Alumni Center. University of Missouri, Columbia.

Walton, Anthony. "The Hardheaded Romantic." *Brown Alumni Magazine.* March/April 2001, pp. 42–49.

————. "Introduction: Sacred Geometry." *Worcester Review* 3, nos. 1 & 2 (2014): 83–123.

Wilenz, Tim, and Tom Weatherly. *Natural Process: An Anthology of New Black Poetry.* Hill and Wang, 1970.

Williams, Sherley Anne. *Give Birth to Brightness: A Thematic Study in Neo-Black Literature.* Dial Press, 1972.

Williams, William Carlos. *In the American Grain.* New Directions Books, 1956.

Young, Kevin. *Ardency: A Chronicle of the Amistad Rebels.* Knopf, 2011.

INDEX